THE PUPPET PRINCE

For Laura Lee
With love and God's
Blessing - your friend
La Vonne Chung
7-12-17

LAVONNE CHUNG

ISBN: 1539835324
ISBN 13: 9781539835325

CHAPTER 1

Maxwell gently lifted Marion's arm and slipped silently from between the silky sheets, the moonlight reflecting off his lean naked body. He moved gingerly across the room toward the veranda bathed in elegant silver light. The sea lapped softly against the rocky shore. Maxwell lay down on the full length of the chaise offering himself as a sacrifice to the full moon, basking in its glory. He locked his hands behind his head his mop of hair still tangled from the grasping strokes of Marion's insistent hands and looked up into the clear night sky. A million stars flickered and twinkled, winking at him as he lay naked as Adam in the Garden of Eden. Peace enveloped him as he allowed himself to sink into the softness of the lounge beneath him. "How long will this peace last?" he wondered. "Will I let them down?" "Have they chosen the right man?" These and many other questions made endless circuits in his mind as he contemplated the awesome purpose that his life was destined to fulfill. He closed his eyes, the bright moon still a glow beneath his heavy lids. He pondered his predicament and wondered how it would all end. The beginning was already becoming a fuzzy memory after all these years. "Was it real? Did it really happen?" Yes it was real, although many times, like tonight, Maxwell could scarcely believe it himself.

For Maxwell it had all started with the first international crisis after being sworn in for a second term as President of the United States of America. It was at that time he had been made aware of a plot to take control of the nations of the world. Many individual nations had espoused that goal in the past, but it was quite another matter to have proof that just such a takeover was actually in progress.

Suddenly it seemed as though it were all happening again and those long past events became as crystal clear as his and Marion's love making an hour ago.

George Middleton, Maxwell's Advisor in Chief, had set up a top-secret meeting with the head of International Security.

"Maxwell, ISA chief, Paul Roberts."

Maxwell extended his hand in a friendly greeting, "Glad to meet you. Welcome to America."

"Thank you, sir," said the strikingly handsome, tall young man in a deep, thick brogue.

The president motioned to the comfortable chairs positioned in front of the fireplace. "Sit down please, gentlemen. Would either of you care for a brandy or perhaps coffee or tea?" The men were seated and served and the meeting began in earnest.

Time slipped silently away. Maxwell leaned wearily back in his chair, locked his hands thoughtfully behind his head and asked, "Are you sure? I mean *positively* sure, that the facts you have just revealed to me are *absolutely* true?"

The two men eyed each other in penetrating calm.

"Mr. President, I stake my life on it. The assassination is planned. The hit is to take place between your hotel and McCormick Center. We know the exact location of the hit. We know the identity of the hit man, even the exact window from which the fatal shot will be fired."

Maxwell's brow furrowed in thought. He shook his head in disbelief. "I will have to cancel my appearance," he said.

Paul Roberts cleared his throat before continuing, "I haven't told you everything as yet, sir. You *will* go to Chicago as planned and you *will* be assassinated as planned."

"Now wait just a god damned minute!" Maxwell croaked pushing himself out of his chair and spilling his brandy, "I'm a dedicated man, but this is preposterous."

George placed his hand on Maxwell's shoulder and pushed him gently back into his chair, "Sit down. It isn't quite like it seems. Let Paul explain."

The President was visibly shaken. He turned and looked at his trusted advisor suspiciously. "Just what in hell do you know about all this George?" he demanded.

"Enough to know that Paul knows what he is talking about." George refilled Maxwell's glass before resuming his seat.

"May I continue, sir?" the agent inquired.

Maxwell drained his brandy before nodding his consent.

"Russia has your Vice President in its pocket," he said, producing documents to substantiate his claim. "They know you are the only man on the face of the earth that has enough guts to resist them at the risk of an all out war. I don't need to brief you on the degeneration of the American public. The average American voter isn't looking at the issues. They are voting personality. Charisma is what wins elections these days. You've got it and much more. You mean business and they know it! Their four-point plan was right on schedule till you came along Mr. President. First Asia, second Eastern Europe, third Africa, and finally the Americas."

George grinned with pride at Maxwell. "They certainly underestimated you when they tried to pull that shit in the Caribbean."

"If their progress is short circuited at this stage it could defeat their ultimate goal," Paul interjected.

"Be specific," Maxwell snapped.

Paul Roberts placed a thick file folder on the coffee table before Maxwell. "This is an outline of a detailed plan to overthrow the United States and ultimately gain control of the entire world." He pulled out several charts. "Notice the dates involved in particular. Now look at the same timetable for the World Economic Community. Every date lines up all across the board. They have calculated precisely WEC's every move. These WEC plans are classified, top secret documents. The metric system isn't completely in place as yet but notice this," he pointed to a series of numbers, "notice how the KGB has pegged all our projection dates, even World Day, which is nearly twenty years in the future. The database in Brussels is right on target along with world banking and our space program." He put down the folder. "Cunning these Russians. They know all our plans and have made their own to coincide. They are allowing us to do all the organizational groundwork for them, using our talents, draining our pocket books. Cunning as hell. They plan to rush off the field with the trophy!"

"I still don't see where I fit in."

"The most crucial aspect of their plan is facilitating the moral decay of America," Paul explained. "You, Mr. President, have been like a shot in the arm to this country. Segregation is a thing of the past. You are waging *and* winning the war on drugs. Your Youth Corps Program is a stunning success and the economy has never looked so good. You are a natural leader and have won the hearts of your people. Not only your own people here in America, but the nations of the world are captivated by your leadership."

"Russia is losing ground fast," George added in a matter-of-fact tone.

"So they plan to assassinate me?"

"Yes."

Paul Roberts stood, unlocked his briefcase and took out an oversized envelope. He pushed it across the table to Maxwell. George also got up and prepared to leave.

"That's it then?" Maxwell looked dumbstruck. They were leaving!

"We'll be in touch," assured Paul extending his hand. "In the meantime, old chap, mum's the word."

CHAPTER 2

Maxwell stood before the fireplace looking intently at the envelope in his hand. He sat down in a nearby chair and carefully opened it. He read the contents slowly and thoroughly before folding it into a familiar triangular shape. Taking careful aim he let it sail smoothly into the dying embers. "Bulls eye," he said softly as he watched the flames leap hungrily to life consuming the message.

The door opened suddenly and his children came bounding into the room. Six-year-old Leslie threw herself into her father's arms, "Time to eat PaPa," she announced. Maxwell stood Leslie on her feet and reached for the toddler swooping him up high in the air. Max proceeded to clap his little hands in glee as they marched dutifully to the dining room.

Much later, after the children had been put to bed, Marion sat brushing her hair, studying her husband's countenance in the mirror. Something was bothering him. Maxwell was making an unsuccessful attempt to read a financial report. She put down her brush and went to his chair. Kneeling before him she pulled the report into his lap and looked up into his dark troubled eyes. "What's bothering you, dearest," she asked simply.

"How perceptive is this woman I married," he thought, taking her small hands into his own. "I do have something I must tell you," he said heavily.

After Maxwell finished telling her about his meeting with George and the ISA Chief, Marion was pale and visibly shaken.

"But what does it all mean?" she asked, her eyes searching his in desperation. "What are we going to do?"

"I don't have all the answers yet. I guess we will find out more when we go to Mount Weather on Saturday. Marion, I'm sorry about our trip to Camp David. I know how much you were looking forward to our weekend there."

"Well, at least we'll be together. Maxwell, are you *sure* you were instructed to bring the children? Maybe they are going to hide us or something," she mumbled. Marion had a curious habit of thinking out loud.

"That could be it," he said, drawing her into his lap and the comfort of his arms. Maxwell didn't tell her that Roberts had assured him that the assassination would take place as planned. He knew there were a few surprises in the poke but why worry her? He tightened his grip as she snuggled closer.

Very early on Saturday morning Maxwell, Marion, and the two children left the White House by limousine while at the same moment four figures, a man, a woman, and two children were seen boarding the presidential helicopter bound for Camp David.

Little Max flattened his tiny nose against the tinted glass, looking up as the familiar chopping sounds' crescendo then began to fade. "Coppa," he giggled.

The driver pulled the sleek limo out of the White House Complex and turned up Constitution Avenue past the Lincoln Memorial, by-passing Arlington National Cemetery. Soon they were speeding north on the Leesburg Pike leaving the city far behind.

The hour or so drive through the pristine countryside was so occupied by Max's antics that they barely noticed when the car pulled up to the security entrance of the gigantic underground complex and were ushered into its inner sanctum. Their driver opened the door and the four of them tumbled out into the huge concrete vault. Marion brushed Leslie's hair from her face and adjusted Max's clothes amid squeals of echoing protest.

The President picked up his son and retrieved Leslie's hand and they moved to the nearby elevator, their heels making musical clicks on the concrete as they walked. They stepped inside and the elevator doors closed before they were plunged rapidly down into the depths of the earth. The swift dropping sensation and the slight bobbing as they came to their destination gave Max yet another reason to giggle, and this time he was joined by his sister. The door opened and they emerged into a tastefully appointed reception area. The receptionist, a sharp looking Navel officer, smiled warmly and picked up the phone on her desk. "The President and Mrs. Hurst have arrived, sir," she announced.

A wall panel slid silently aside and George Middleton strode into the room.

"Marion, my dear. Maxwell! Welcome to Mount Weather." He shook hands with the President and placed an affectionate arm around Marion drawing her into the room.

"Marion, I want you to meet Paul Roberts. Paul is with the ISA. Paul, may I present the first lady of the USA, Marion Hurst?"

"How do you do, Mr. Roberts?" she asked politely.

Paul took her extended hand in his with surprising gentleness. A bit star struck by her pale beauty, he found himself fascinated by her brilliant blue eyes and her demure manner. "It is my pleasure to meet you at last, Mrs. Hurst," he said with sincerity as he released her hand and turned his attention to the children. "So this is Max and Leslie, I presume?"

The President proudly presented the two children. "Leslie. Max. Say hello to the chief!"

At the same moment the panel slid to the side a second time and a pert looking woman in a Navel uniform entered. George introduced her as Lieutenant Kirkland and explained that she would be entertaining the children. Marion cast an anxious glance at the exit as her precious children went dutifully out with the stranger.

"Don't worry, Marion," George said patting her hand reassuringly, "the Lieutenant is wonderful with children, they will be perfectly safe."

The four sat at a large round table in comfortable armchairs. George opened a folder that lay on the table before him and began to read a brief of the plot involving the President. Marion's eyes widened in disbelief as the details were exposed. Her mind reeled in incomprehension as George tried to explain a proposed counter plot. George paused momentarily to allow her to digest what he had just told her and then looked her squarely in the eyes and asked, "Do you have any questions before I continue?" She suddenly realized that this meeting was for *her* benefit!

Marion's lip quivered and her voice broke as she asked, "Am I to under-stand, George, that the CIA and the ISA are aware of a plot to kill my hus-band when he goes to Chicago in August?" She plunged on before George could answer. "*And* am I to understand that Maxwell is to go just as planned and that nothing will be done to stop this horrible thing from happening?"

Paul Roberts responded, his brogue thickening with compassion, "In ef-fect, yes. That *is* what we are saying, Mrs. Hurst."

"Well, not exactly," George hurriedly added, "We do have the counter plot."

Maxwell reached for Marion's hand as George continued.

"You see, we intend to pull the shooter and replace him with our own man."

Marion gasped in horror.

"Calm down, Marion. Our man is an expert marksman. Maxwell won't be killed. We have to draw blood to make this work *and* we must have your complete cooperation!"

Marion tried to protest but George rushed on, "You see, the President will be dead only in the eyes of the world."

She stared at George in disbelief then shifted her eyes to her husband who, she suddenly realized, knew about this plan and had already agreed to it. A sick feeling swept over her body, the blood draining from her beautiful face. She faced the three men sitting before her. Maxwell was moving quickly behind her chair placing gentle comforting hands on her shoulders. George was handing her a glass of water and as she drank the cool liquid the reality of what they were suggesting began to seep slowly into her understanding.

The men waited in polite silence until it was apparent that Marion had re-gained her composure. Setting her glass on the table she reached for Maxwell's hand, still on her shoulder, and gave him a reassuring signal. He took his seat beside her once more. Marion's eyes fixed on George. Dear old George. Could she trust him? She felt he would never do anything to hurt them.

"What's next then?" she whispered.

The men breathed an almost audible sigh of relief. Paul looked at Marion with admiration. "What a woman," he thought.

"The details are still being refined," George said, "But the gist of the plan is that Maxwell will only *appear* to be dead. It will be your job to convince the world that he is. Only a handful of people know about this. This is Classified, Top Secret—*the very top*. We have access to a remote island in the Aegean Sea. Maxwell will be secretly taken there where he must remain until phase three of the master plan can be implemented. The less you know of all this the better," he cautioned. "We realize what a tremendous sacrifice we are asking of you and your family but believe me, Marion, it is for the good of mankind that we ask it." George paused in thoughtful consideration and then added, "No, more than that. It is for the preservation of the *world* that we ask it."

Marion had listened intently and many questions bombarded her mind but one took precedence over the rest. "You mentioned a phase three. I assume then that there is a phase one and two? What sort of time frame are we talking about?"

George looked at Paul uncomfortably. "That's the hard part," he admitted. "We could be talking about twenty years or more."

"What?" she shrieked. "That's impossible! You expect us to carry on a charade like this for twenty years? For the rest of our lives?" Marion jumped to her feet, overturning her chair and pushing Maxwell away as he tried to restrain her. "Crazy! You're *all* crazy!" she screamed as she ran from the room.

Maxwell looked at the bewildered men. "She'll come around. You can count on her," he reassured them. "I hope so, Maxwell," George said quietly. "I certainly hope so." And Maxwell was certainly right.

Chapter 3

Days turned into weeks and weeks into months. The eighteenth of August loomed ominously before them. It was Sunday, August fifteenth. This would be their last public appearance together as a family. They shared a special, almost sanctifying mood as they entered Saint Matthews Cathedral that morning.

The priests moved slowly and purposefully up the aisle followed by the bishop in golden finery. They moved in perfect rhythm to the arias of the choir boys singing the introit in crystal a cappella strains. This was the Feast of Assumption with all the color and pageantry that attended a High Mass. Even little Max sat quietly beside his sister, minus the usual wiggles.

Marion, scarcely able to concentrate on the Bishop's words, felt suspended in motion as she found herself moving with the others toward the alter while the bishop chanted, "Behold the Lamb of God who takes away the sins of the world."

Her own response, "Lord, I am not worthy," seemed redundant when she really wanted to cry out, "Oh God, give me a sign that everything is going to be all right!"

Maxwell was kneeling beside her at the communion rail, head bent in prayer. She tilted her head back slightly to receive the Eucharist and when she did her eyes rested on the statue of the Virgin Mary. Her face etched in sorrow, seemed to be gazing directly down upon them. Marion could not take her eyes off that lovely face. Then something strange happened. The face of the Virgin began to glow and Marion could have sworn that her mouth had softened into a slight, sweet smile. Marion's heart was mysteriously warmed and she left the altar in peace knowing that what ever was about to happen to them was within the will of God.

They left the Cathedral like a normal family, hand in hand, the children between them. They spent the afternoon in their secret place: a cool, shady garden in the heart of Arlington. They were hardly ever discovered in this place; and if they were recognized by the public, Secret Service Agents were always nearby to assure them of their privacy. They often partook of a picnic lunch in this quiet solitude surrounded by rows and rows of silent white stone sentinels. It was the kind of afternoon where secrets were exchanged in whispers and the silence was broken only by the singing of the birds and the occasional high pitched squeals and giggles of Max as he romped with his daddy on the soft green grass carpet.

Later that evening after the children had been tucked into their beds, the bags packed, and the final briefing concluded, Maxwell and Marion sought the seclusion of their chambers. Marion was in bed, curled up under a pale yellow comforter. Maxwell came to sit beside her. "Are you ready for tomorrow, dearest," he asked gently.

Marion thought about tonight's briefing which was one of dozens. At one briefing they had actually practiced their parts: which way to turn, how to fall.

"I think so," she said. "Yes, I believe I am," she added with conviction, remembering the incident at Mass. She reached up to touch his dear face as he bent to kiss her. "I'll miss you, Maxwell."

"We'll be together again soon," he promised as he gathered her into his arms.

A seemingly endless night gave birth to a hot and muggy August day. They enjoyed a long, unhurried breakfast with the children, savoring each moment. Time was running out.

"Keep still. Let mommy tuck in your shirt."

Max squirmed to get away.

"Kiss Daddy good-bye." Marion said with a heavy heart as she watched Maxwell scoop up his son for a farewell hug. The most difficult and painful part of all was that no one could know the truth—not even the children, at least not until they were old enough to be trusted. Leslie pushed in for her share and Maxwell sat down placing one child on each knee.

George knocked softly on the door just as Maxwell was planting a kiss on each waiting cheek. "I hate to break this up, but we'd better get going."

One last hard squeeze and then he and Marion were outside. The door closed behind them. Tears spilled unchecked down Marion's cheeks. Maxwell tightened his grip on her waist and never looked back. Chicago seemed an eternity into the future.

CHAPTER 4

The Motorcade left O'Hare International Airport and nosed on to the Kennedy Expressway right on schedule. The President and Mrs. Hurst would have plenty of time to unwind before the formal reception planned by the mayor.

Security was heavy at the posh Michigan Avenue hotel. The penthouse, with its locked doors, was a haven where they could be completely alone. Marion wandered out onto the balcony to enjoy the view. Lake Michigan appeared to be sprinkled with jewels in the full glare of the August sun. Maxwell came and stood close behind her wrapping her in the security of his arms as if to protect her from the morrow and all the uncertainty connected with it.

"I wish we could stay here forever, Maxwell."

"And just what would we do if we stayed here forever, Mrs. Hurst?"

"I could think of a few good ideas," she teased turning toward him.

"Well, *I* think we should take a short nap and then get ready for this evening."

"Good idea," she said, taking his hand and leading him back into the apartment.

Sometime later George arrived to accompany them to the reception. "Are you two ready?" he inquired. Marion was a vision in pink satin, her blonde tresses pulled back in a stylish chignon. She wore little makeup and her blue eyes and her sparkling smile complimented her natural beauty.

"You look lovely my dear. As usual," he added with a deep bow.

Marion returned a feigned curtsy, "Why, thank you, Sir George!"

"What do you think, George?" Maxwell asked as he strode into the room, "Don't we make a handsome couple?"

"Absolutely smashing! The most handsome couple I know."

The dinner reception was being held in the Rose Room, a lovely hall with a fitting name. The place was a virtual Rose Garden. At once Marion was reminded of the uncomfortable smell of a funeral parlor and she clung tightly to Maxwell's arm. He seemed relaxed, smiling broadly, unaware of her discomfort.

"Mr. President. Mrs. Hurst. Welcome to Chicago," the gregarious Mayor Walker said as he pumped Maxwell's hand vigorously. "What a pleasure this is. You remember my wife, Valerie?"

Valerie flashed a brilliant smile-flashy enough to match the brilliance of her metallic gown. "Maxwell, darling. How good to see you again." She took the President's arm to escort him to the banquet table. "How are you, Marion dear?" she asked as she sailed past. A helpless expression crossed Maxwell's face as he looked back over his shoulder at his perturbed wife. Marion reluctantly took the arm that the paunchy mayor offered and was dutifully seated beside him at the table.

Maxwell and Valerie seemed enthralled in livid conversation, intermittent with Valerie's indecorous laughter. The evening seemed endless although not completely boring. Marion felt she had received a crash course in cross breeding orchids. However, when the meal was ended and the formalities finished, she was more than willing to say goodnight to the botanical Mayor Walker. Maxwell, on the other hand, seemed much less eager to leave the company of the amusing Valerie Walker.

"I hate these damned affairs," Marion muttered to herself as they waited for the elevator. "What was so hilarious anyway?" she demanded punching her husband hard in the side with her elbow.

"Hey that hurt! What did I do?"

Marion swept past him into the suite and headed for the bedroom. Maxwell was in hot pursuit.

"Honey let's not be ridiculous," he pleaded. "Valerie is just a good looking, entertaining wench—that's all. Can I help it if entertaining wenches find me attractive? Come on," Maxwell pleaded, folding his arms around his wife and holding her tightly to him, "You are the one and only love of my life. And don't you forget it!"

All hostility drained from her. Resistance was useless as she yielded to his embrace.

CHAPTER 5

The day dawned: a carbon copy of the one just past. Hot and humid. An ominous haze lingered over the city of Chicago. Maxwell and Marion were far from ready to face what lay ahead.

"Leslie, give Max the phone now. Yes, Daddy loves you too. Bye, bye, sweetheart. Max? How are you, sport?" Maxwell listened to his son's giddy chatter, his eyes filling with tears. "Yes, Daddy will bring you something from Kago," he lied. "You be a good boy now. Daddy loves you." Placing the receiver in the cradle he wondered if *anything* was worth the sacrifice he was about to make. "How can I ever survive without them?" he wondered, seeking comfort in Marion's arms.

Suddenly George was in the room. "Let's get going," he said, pulling them out of the security of the moment and pushing them out into the vastness of the future.

They rode in an open limousine typical of Maxwell's trust in the American Public. Mayor Walker and Valerie sat just ahead of them. The limo slid easily from Michigan Avenue onto Monroe then turned right again on to Lake Shore Drive before heading east toward McCormick Place where the convention was being held.

Marion clung tightly to Maxwell's arm. They had not been told where or when the assassination attempt would occur only that it would happen during the ride to McCormick Place. Fans peppered the landscape. Throngs of people crowded the curbs reaching out and waving, their smiling faces non-threatening. Maxwell smiled and waved in return knowing that any one of them could be the shooter.

Marion heard the shot ring out and at the same time saw the stunned look on her husband's face as he slumped toward her. Blood erupted from his wounded head spattering her face and suit. She screamed his name as the mayor and Valerie looked on in horror. Secret Service men were suddenly on the limo shouting commands.

Marion tore at her jacket. Removing it, she carefully wrapped his bleeding head as she had been instructed, shielding their private agony from the prying eyes of the public especially the vulture reporters who would be everywhere with flashing, mechanical eyes. Maxwell seemed lifeless as he lay in Marion's arms as the limo raced wildly toward nearby Saint Joseph Hospital. The emergency room staff met them and carefully lifted Maxwell on to a gurney.

The jacket Marion had so frantically tried to keep in place fell to one side exposing a gaping wound above his left ear. She stared down into wide, open, lifeless eyes. "Oh my God," she cried, "They've actually killed him!"

At least ten white flashes sent her into a mindless rage. Her last memory of that fateful day was hearing herself scream Maxwell's name while swinging her pocketbook wildly at gawking insensitive reporters.

As the anesthesia began to wear off Maxwell began to stir. He had one hell-of-a-whopping headache. Moaning groggily he reached up and felt the bandage that encased his head. "My iron mask," he thought while trying to peer out into the darkened room through thick peepholes. "I'm lucky I still have a head," he mused. "Wow! What a marksman."

A shaft of light split the darkness, "Awake yet, Mr. Howard?" the nurse asked.

Maxwell murmured softly, not quite sure if he was ready to join the land of the living, especially since that living was to be so drastically and suddenly altered.

The decision was made for him, however, when a perky young nurse tilted the wand on the blinds and the sun came streaming into the room. He blinked his eyes in pain as they adjusted to the brilliant light.

"There, isn't that better?" she asked. "I'll bring your supper. You might want to turn on the television. While you were in surgery this morning some kook shot the President!"

After she left he picked up the remote and the picture came instantly into focus. It was a shock to see Marion's image fill the screen. She was covered in blood, wrestling with the medics to keep her jacket wound around his wounded head. He watched as they whisked him away leaving her standing alone and bewildered. His heart ached for her. "I'll make this up to you darling," he solemnly promised.

The newscaster's voice droned on, "Again, the top story. President Maxwell Hurst was assassinated this morning in Chicago, Illinois, as he sat in an open limousine on his way to McCormick Center. It is thought to be the work of a lone assassin. No suspects have been arrested." He went on to detail the funeral that was being planned, as the nation prepared to mourn a fallen leader.

Maxwell was awed at the apparent devotion of the citizens of the United States but it was mind boggling as he gradually became cognizant of his personal popularity in other nations. He had been aware that his leadership was more than noteworthy in many countries throughout the world, but this—this was phenomenal! He saw pictures of his grief stricken wife and children. He switched off the television.

The nurse returned with his meal. "Not interested in the news?" she asked.

"It depresses me," he mumbled.

He was beginning to go stir crazy. "A week in this place will drive a man to drink," he thought, "A well person, that is."

Flowers had been delivered that morning from Carla. Maxwell was enjoying the flowers while contemplating the mystery of who this Carla might be when a hospital volunteer brought in the mail. "A card for you, Mr. Howard," the young girl announced cheerfully.

Opening the envelope carefully, he read, "Hope you're feeling better. See you Tuesday, Love Carla."

Tuesday finally arrived and so did she. He had just finished his lunch when the door opened and she was in his arms. Laughing, crying, kissing. So relieved to feel his flesh on hers. Count his fingers and toes.

"Maxwell! The funeral was *awful*. It was so *real*! Before he knew what was happening she was in his bed. "Make me believe it didn't really happen," she begged.

"Honey," he laughed, "The nurse might come in. Besides it's against the rules!"

"No she won't," Marion whispered, "there's a guard outside."

"Hang the rules," he said pulling her close.

Later Marion pulled on her skirt and buttoned it at the waist. "I won't see you again, not here anyway. They are moving you soon." She made a face, "Then they can remove that awful bandage!"

"Oh, you don't like my mug, huh kid?" he teased in Bogart-style, rubbing his rough bandaged face against her soft cheek. "Well me neither kid," he confessed, "It itches like hell and I *know* I need a shave!"

They lay side-by-side in the narrow bed and talked about the children and the future and all too soon the afternoon was spent. Marion cried for their lost life wondering if she could cope with what was to come. At least she hadn't lost him completely. For a short agonizing time after the assassination she imagined that she truly had.

Chapter 6

Mr. Howard was dismissed three days later with his head still encased in the gauze mask. An agent picked him up and accompanied him to O'Hare where both men boarded a plane bound for Greece. Very little was said between them; both were following separate top-secret orders.

As they departed the plane a middle-aged gentleman approached them.

Dressed in black with his shiny dark hair slicked back behind his ears he almost qualified as New York City mafia material.

"Mr. Howard I presume?" he inquired, extending his hand. "My name is Rolph Venzelos.

I'll be taking over from here." He said turning toward the other man.

"Right. I'll be off then. Nice chatting with you Mr. Howard." He tipped his hat and disappeared into the crowd.

Rolph maneuvered the car through the busy winding streets of Athens, heading toward the port city of Piraeus. It was impossible to tell where one city ended and the other began. The brilliant blue of the Aegean Sea nipped and dug into the shore line causing a now you see it now you don't sort of journey. One last hairpin curve accomplished with screeching tires and the port lay before them in pristine splendor.

Maxwell was more than relieved when they reached the dock and prepared to board the yacht.

"The roads are a bit hazardous here, sir," Rolph apologized.

"I'll be okay. I always green up on mountain roads. How far are we going by sea?"

"Do you get sea sick?"

"No, thank God for that."

"Not far, a couple of hours to the south. Thera is a privately owned island in the Kikladhes. Not much to it but *very* private. If you would like to take a nap or freshen up your cabin is just through here."

As soon as the cabin door was shut behind him Maxwell fell exhausted onto the bunk and went sound asleep.

A persistent tapping on the door and Rolph's cheerful voice roused Maxwell from somewhere deep inside himself.

"Mr. President. We are nearly there. Ready to emerge, sir?" he asked snipping the air with a pair of sharp surgical scissors.

"Am I ever!" Maxwell exclaimed rolling himself into a sitting position. He tilted his head exposing a captive ear lobe.

Rolph went to work carefully clipping and unwinding the gauze until Maxwell was finally free of it. He stood back to look at the unkempt bearded face. A face hardly recognizable as the now famous President Maxwell Hurst, fallen hero of the nations.

Rolph managed a smart salute then left the cabin. Maxwell ran his fingers through the stubble that was the beginning of a new head of hair that promised to be as thick, healthy *and* as unmanageable as ever.

The boat was moored to the dock before he finished his grooming and when he emerged from the cabin shaved and dressed Maxwell sucked in his breath at the view before him. "*Not much to it?*" Rolph could not have been referring to this villa that seemed wedded to the cliff on which it was built. The dazzling whitewashed exterior became one with the craggy limestone bluffs, the burnt orange of the tiled roof made startling contrast. Above and behind was a terraced garden. The setting sun filtering through the dusky green of the olive trees appeared as a lace mantle overshadowing the only structure on the tiny barren island. Rolph led the way from the dock up the wide inviting entrance to the villa.

Huge green ferns in Grecian urns lined the marble steps leading up to the veranda where the house staff stood respectfully awaiting their introduction to the new master of Villa Rose.

An attractive matronly person of perhaps fifty stepped forward. "Welcome to Villa Rose, Mr. President. It is certainly our pleasure to serve you," she said with the slightest curtsy.

"Mr. President. Martha Truelove. Martha is the house manager," Rolph began the introductions.

Maxwell nodded and smiled pleasantly at the India born Englishwoman.

"And this is Carmen our upstairs maid. Carmen livens things up around here." Maxwell looked approvingly at the lovely young Grecian girl as she too welcomed him to Villa Rose.

"Joseph wears two hats: butler and gardener. He is a fine gardener. The best! We believe you will agree when you tour the rose gardens. As to his abilities as your butler that remains to be seen," Rolph laughed.

Joseph who spoke in broken English was a slight, short Dutchman. He grinned from ear to ear as he shifted his hat into his left hand in order to take the one offered to him by the President.

"Last, but certainly not least, we are very fortunate to have Stan Newton whom we here at Villa Rose consider the best chef in any country of the world. Stan will have the opportunity to prove his claim to fame shortly and I'm willing to bet *very* big bucks that you will agree with me, Mr. President."

"I'm sure I will," Maxwell said shaking the tall black man's hand. "It's good to meet you. Good to meet all of you," he said smiling at each of them. "And please, do call me Maxwell. I'm sure we will come to be very good friends in time."

Indeed they had become a close knit little group. An odd lot—six people willing to dedicate what seemed like a lifetime to what each considered the highest honor under heaven—to bring global order to a disorderly world! For the house staff it meant doing all the menial, monotonous everyday tasks that become woven into the lining of an ornate tapestry. As for Maxwell he still wasn't quite sure what it all meant for him but he had implicit faith in the men who had brought him this far and it was this that convinced him of the validity of his involvement. Little did Maxwell realize the extent of the tapestry being woven. Nor could he envision how central he was to its completion.

Rolph on the other hand had no doubt about his role in all this. He was a believer, body, soul, and spirit. A patriot willing to give up everything for the cause; in fact, he had. Mother, father, brothers, and lover—all believed him to be lost at sea. He would never be found.

CHAPTER 7

As it turned out, things had fallen rather smoothly into place. The first weeks and months had consisted of intense training sessions with Rolph proving to be an expert teacher. A network of three strategically located workstations was the main ingredient for synchronizing global unity. Under the code names of A, B, and C these three supercomputers were linked by a single secret satellite called the "eye". A was located in Virginia at Mount Weather; B was in Brussels, Belgium; and C was installed in the caverns beneath Villa Rose. These computers composed a top-secret network so impregnable that any leaks could only originate from within the ranks. B known as the beast because of its massive storage system was the central control. C was a speech-activated marvel and "she" was affectionately referred to as "CC". With Rolph's expertise and teaching skills Maxwell soon had his ABCs down pat!

George's image filled the monitor, "How's the weather over there?" he asked.

"Wonderful! Blue and balmy as usual."

"Brr," George shivered. "Snowed in here. I'm looking forward to a reprieve. Is everything set for our meeting on Thursday?"

"Every thing is set," Maxwell assured him.

"Good. See you on Thursday then."

George's image was replaced by a colorful holographic display of swirling lines and soothing music. CC was at rest and this would be the last contact until the meeting. Maxwell could scarcely believe that six months had passed so quickly. He was looking forward to Thursday with much more than official interest. George was his very good friend and he enjoyed the company of the handsome good humored Roberts immensely. His relationship with Rolph was evolving slowly as they worked side by side with CC but in spite of that Maxwell often felt isolated and lonely.

Three short blasts of the ship's horn announced the arrival of the "Sea Witch". Thursday had arrived at last. Maxwell stood on the veranda that overlooked the dock watching as Rolph welcomed their guests to Villa Rose. George spotted his friend on the veranda and quickly ascended the graceful sloping marble stairs to the main entrance. The two men embraced in a back slapping bear hug.

"Damn it's good to see you!" George exclaimed.

Paul had reached them and stood to one side smiling broadly. "You *are* looking good, Mr. President."

"Thank you, Paul," Maxwell said shaking the younger man's hand. "It is good to see you again. How are things in Brussels?"

"Fine. Doing just fine."

"Well I hope you men are hungry because you are about to experience the treat of a lifetime. Stan has got to be the best chef in the business!"

George punched Maxwell playfully in the mid-section. "Now that you've brought it up, old boy, you do look a bit paunchy."

Maxwell patted himself proudly. "A walking testimony. Yes sir that's me!"

After a long relaxing meal Maxwell's guests had to agree: Stan was the best. When the laureates were concluded the conversation turned to politics as usual.

Maxwell got up to refresh his drink. "I see Burke is muddling through okay. He certainly is performing better than I would have predicted when he was my Vice President. He shows quite a bit of spark as a matter-of-fact."

"Show is the right word," Paul said, grinding out his cigarette in apparent disgust. "He jumps when his string is pulled!"

"Don't we all?" George asked, looking absently at the smoldering butt in the ashtray.

Maxwell shot George an uneasy glance but he wasn't looking. He stood up. "We'd better turn in, gentlemen. I know you are bushed and we have a lot of work to do tomorrow."

A short while later after each had retired to his own quarters Maxwell heard a light tap on his door. George handed him a manila envelope. "Nearly forgot this," he said grinning sheepishly. "Pleasant dreams."

Alone again he dumped the contents of the envelope on his desk. Several pictures, a disc, and a letter fell out. Maxwell shuffled through the pictures little Max grinned up at him with sweet innocent eyes and toothless Leslie looked every bit of the minx that she was. Marion's letter brought tears—her loneliness enlarging and converging with his own.

"It won't be long now, darling," she had written. "George keeps telling me to be patient-that you and I and the children will be reunited soon. I long for that day, my dearest. Love, Marion."

He popped the disc into his PC and watched as the children romped and played in the snow blanketing the lawn of the Bar Harbor hide-a-way. When he did get to bed, Maxwell slept fitfully dreaming of Marion and the children and of Acadia, his boyhood home on the other side of the world. Morning seemed an eternity in coming.

"Ah, so this is your baby?" Paul rubbed his palm across the smooth shiny top of the super computer. "Some hardware," he said admiringly. CC was the newest of the three and had infinite capabilities. "These machines never cease to amaze me. Like a bottomless pit we will never delve the depth of their usefulness."

"Why, thank you, Mr. Roberts," CC responded in a soft feminine voice. "I find you most attractive also."

Maxwell chuckled when Paul realized that Rolph, who was seated at the console, had initiated her response.

"Enough fun and games," George said with a smile. "Let's get down to business, shall we? Have you got the flow charts ready Rolph?"

Rolph punched a few keys and the console hummed as information was received, digested, organized, and regurgitated. In seconds, information that had taken hours, days, months, and even years to compile was at his fingertips.

WORD: World Order through Religious Discipline. That was the plan in a nutshell. Consolidate the three great religions of the world in order to regulate behavior and control population; hence the basis of stable government could be realized. Of course some freedom would necessarily have to be exchanged for peace. But the peace of the planet, after all, was the most important consideration in the long run.

Much progress was being made by the United Nations and international cooperation was being achieved in most areas of the world. Even Russia seemed to be lining up nicely. Most nations had followed China's example in controlling population by regulating the occurrence of live births. With the birth rate down and agricultural production up the hunger issue was being brought under control. The covert plans of the new system were being implemented on every level of human need bringing about cooperation and goodwill between Nations. Even the super powers assumed a friendly stance—signing treaties, limiting and abolishing arms, embracing a theology of peace—or so it seemed.

George held the thick folder of printed matter aloft. "Gentlemen," he said, "The WORD is ready for our final approval. As you know, the plan requires that we choose a suitable spokesperson for the ecclesiastical administration of the WORD. This person, known as the Bishop must have the ability to unite the citizens of the nations when the time is ripe. Several well known figures have been groomed for this position. It is our task to make the final decision."

Rolph's fingers flicked purposefully across the keys. CC responded in her soft commanding voice, "Gentlemen, the candidates that will appear for your consideration are each qualified to serve our purpose. Please evaluate all information carefully."

The face of a world famous Christian evangelist filled the screen along with a print out of pertinent information. She was known worldwide for her huge healing crusades. Her philosophy of a theocracy would easily qualify her for indoctrination. Her age was against her. She would be close to ninety in the projected year of consummation.

The bearded stern looking descendant of the famous Ghandi and a renowned Rabbi were equally qualified.

The final candidate came as a pleasant surprise to Maxwell. Jefferson Brandon Richards was a longstanding friend, their association dating back to freedom fighting days of the past. Jeff had been and still was an avid civil rights activist, capturing the devotion of the world's poor and oppressed. His youth, his charisma, and his dream of uniting the world in love, peace, and brotherhood were outstanding qualifications for the man of the WORD.

Hours of soul-searching deliberation brought forth a decision. The Bishop of the WORD would be Jeff Richards, a man destined to become the most famous black leader the world would ever embrace. Jeff could have no way of knowing just how much of his personal destiny had been orchestrated by masterful minds using machines like the Beast and CC.

Later relaxing over drinks the four men discussed the wisdom of their choice.

"I hope Jeff isn't overwhelmed by the changes that are about to take place in his life," Maxwell said.

"He'll be fine," George said, putting down his glass. "You are, aren't you?"

"I'm not so sure about that! I'll let you know in about twenty years," Maxwell laughed.

"It might be more difficult for Reverend Richards though," Paul said as he got up to refill his glass.

"How's that?" George asked.

"He won't be aware of the powers that are shaping his future, at least not initially. We may have to find ways to humble him from time to time.

Rolph who had studied the stats on all the candidates assured them, "No need to worry. Richards is a truly great man and great men can handle their destiny." He looked intently at Maxwell and smiled with naked admiration.

Rolph was right. As the years came and went, Jeff seemed unimpressed by his own phenomenal popularity. People from every walk of life and in every country adored him. At the same time the memory of Maxwell Hurst was deliberately and carefully kept fresh and alive creating a larger than life much loved image: a hero. Both men were perfectly suited for what was believed to be a divinely directed destiny.

CHAPTER 8

Rolph and Maxwell were in the cavern working with CC when a message was received from the Beast. The plan for Economic Alignment was nearly a year into implementation. It had been a stormy year. Trade deficits and market crashes had been headline news around the globe and the Economic Community had moved swiftly to control the panic. The fullness of time had now come for those who were molding and shaping the future. The nations were moving swiftly to dissolve their monetary systems in favor of a common trading unit. No more euro, yen, or ruble. The United States, accused of foot dragging, came on board only after the decision was made to retain the dollar as the symbol of the new system.

CC relayed the communication from Brussels: "The European Economic Community has just announced that the cooperation of America has made unanimous the Commission's proposal to dissolve all existing monetary systems in favor of a Universal Trade Board, a common monetary unit, and Intra-Banking between member nations. A prompt approval is expected by the Council of Ministers promoting prosperity and world wide peace."

"Well! That's it then!" Maxwell exclaimed. "History in the making!"

"And we are part of it!" Rolph said in wonderment. "Too bad we have to be stuck way out here in no-man's-land."

"Patience, my friend. Our day is coming."

"You're right," Rolph agreed, "and not a day sooner than planned I expect!"

It had not been surprising how easily the issue of a common language was resolved since most nations had cooperated along these lines for years teaching English as a second language. It only made sense that the most commonly understood language should be chosen as the official language of the new confederacy of nations.

CC's gentle voice filled the chamber once more, "Maxwell, communiqué coming in for you," she announced.

George's smiling face appeared on the monitor, "Good news, Maxwell! Marion has finally agreed to the wedding!"

It was a foolproof plan but when they had presented it to Marion she had balked like a wild mare.

"I will do no such thing!" she had vowed. "I don't care if he *is* the richest man in the world and owns half of Greece including *all* the Islands in the Ageon. Good grief, George! You can't be serious!"

"You are absolutely right, Marion. It's not important that he is the richest man in the world but it is important that he owns Thera, that little chunk of land where Maxwell resides and will reside for a long time to come. This is the only safe way we can unite you two."

Marion had glowered at George, "He's ugly as hell!"

"What do you care? You don't have to live with the man you know."

"He's not a Catholic! He's not anything! The Church won't stand for it." A look of genuine pain crossed her face, "Are you asking me to give up the Church?"

George had underestimated how important this was to them both. He should have known, especially after Maxwell had insisted on importing a priest to the island.

"You can celebrate the Sacraments at Villa Rose with Maxwell. When you are there," he added.

"What do you mean? *When* I am there?" she demanded.

"Well we can't attract too much attention to the island. That should be obvious."

Glaring headlines had announced her ultimate defeat. "MARION HURST TO WED WEALTHY GREEK MANUFACTURER". The world was shocked to have even contemplated such a mismatch. He was accused of robbing the cradle, she of greed and worse. The Church publicly criticized her when it was announced that the two would be united in a civil ceremony.

During those trying months it appeared that Marion suffered a personality warp. She desperately tried to avoid publicity but every time she stepped out into the world some reporter pushed his camera into her face. She often lost her composure and presented an ugly picture to the public further damaging her already tarnished image. Neither George, Maxwell, nor any of the others closely involved would ever know the agonizing toll it took on her. They would never know of the many nights she had sobbed herself to sleep in the mortification of what they had forced her to become.

Maxwell was undergoing a change of his own. He was growing a full beard and mustache. "Quite handsome, I must say," Rolph had said. "Marion may not recognize you let alone the children."

Maxwell was getting so impatient as to be snappy and unpleasant with the staff. They understood and stayed to themselves as much as possible but now he was smiling again and full of good will toward them. Marion had agreed to the wedding plans. That meant that they would be together again soon. He would have her. He would have his children back.

Maxwell would never forget the day they arrived: Mikeal Aristotle and his new bride. They stood on the bow of Mikeal's yacht. Marion waving wildly. The kindly gentleman holding her elbow smiled with pleasure at her gladness. He tipped his cap to Maxwell and winked knowingly. He wouldn't be staying. After all he was on his honeymoon and would be sailing these seas for another three weeks before returning to Villa Rose with the children.

It was as though the ten years since their marriage had never existed and they were again on their honeymoon in Jamaica in the quiet little inn at Ocho Rios. They made love. They enjoyed Stans' lavish dishes in the privacy of their quarters—they walked hand in hand in the beautiful gardens—they made love. They talked as they drank wine together and gently renewed their intimacy—they made love.

CHAPTER 9

In three short weeks Mikeal returned to Villa Rose with the children. The three of them had become fast friends: Leslie, Max, and "Uncle Mike".

It was a strange reunion. Their mother and this vaguely familiar man with a thick beard met them at the dock. Maxwell was so overcome with emotion that it frightened little Max who was almost five.

"Mommy! That man squeezed me too hard," he complained into Marion's ear. He was clinging so tightly to her neck that she had to pry his chubby little fingers free. She took his small face between her hands. "He loves you," she explained simply.

Leslie shielded herself behind her mother peering curiously at this man she felt strangely drawn to—this man, who in time she would come to realize was her natural father.

The following week was a grand time for everyone. Maxwell captured the children's hearts and Mikeal further endeared himself to each of them, especially Marion, who was obligated to leave with him at the end of the week. After a month of "honeymooning" they were expected to return to Athens to attend a host of post-nuptial celebrations designed to entrench Marion's reputation as an international socialite. With Mikeal proudly at her side the new Mrs. Aristotle was presented to Greece and the world.

After diligently exploring the barren extent of the island the children were content to settle into a routine of tutors and homework and all of the ordinary things that comprise the life of a child. Maxwell made sure he had plenty of time to spend with his children. He swam with them every after-noon and often took them fishing or sailing.

Marion was at Thera as much as possible. She never got beyond the agony that gripped her each time she had to leave them and return to her "other life." She would stand on the stern of the yacht and watch as the three people she loved most in the world became tiny dots on the horizon. Mikeal was not a difficult person to share a charade with. He was generous beyond imagina-tion, kind, and considerate. Even his craggy weathered features became dear to her. She had long repented of ever declaring him ugly!

Leslie was never far from her pencil and drawing pad. She saw beauty and poetry in every thing around her: the dusky olive trees with their knots and gnarls, the Rose garden, the sheer white cliffs that imprisoned them, even the lobster pink and steamy on her white china plate. Together Maxwell and Marion would examine her work and laugh or cry as they shared this precious part of their private kingdom, agreeing in their belief that they were nurtur-ing a great artist beneath the clear blue skies of their sheltered villa. The day would come, and they both knew it, when they would have to release this rare little bird into the outside world where she could spread her wings and develop her full potential.

Little Max was an ever-changing enigma. He was intelligent and inquisi-tive, more so than most little boys his age. A few months before his twelfth birthday he had nosed his way into the cavern and surprised Maxwell and Rolph working with CC. That's when the training began. From that moment on wherever Rolph was you would most likely find Max. He was as intrigued by the computer as Rolph if that were possible. He resented having to contin-ue with his other studies but his father insisted and Max dutifully complied.

Max was thirteen and Leslie sixteen when they were told their father's true identity. Neither seemed surprised or shocked as Marion had anticipated. It was as though they each had discovered the missing piece of a long lost puzzle. They admitted they had been haunted by a vague uneasiness in Maxwell's pres-ence, yet each had been irresistibly drawn to him. Now they accepted the fact of his life as easily as they had accepted the fact of his death. Little by little they were given knowledge of the purpose behind it all. This too they accepted.

CHAPTER 10

So the years had come and gone slipping in and out between the months and days as relentlessly as the tide that pounded the rocky shores of their island prison.

Rolph, Paul, George, and Maxwell were close associates. The children and the household staff were always there for Maxwell but the years had been made even more tolerable by his growing friendship with Jeff Richards. Jeff and Maxwell had always been congenial but as Jeff was gradually indoctrinated into the organization the relationship had solidified into something much more than mere friendship.

Jeff's popularity was astounding. His presence at any assembly large or small seemed to crackle with some kind of invisible energy that radiated from him to the crowd. He had the ability to unify people from every race, creed, or station in life, meeting needs on every level. Jeff honestly believed himself to be a chosen instrument in God's plan to bring peace to the world.

Indeed he *was* chosen just as Maxwell was and as they were spun deeper and deeper into the intriguing web of conspiracy—God's conspiracy, or so they believed, to bring the whole world to order and peace—their devotion deepened. Convinced of their mutual destiny they spent endless hours dreaming of, discussing, and desiring the arrival of the new system.

It was now inevitable. There was no turning back. And now as Maxwell lay naked on the deck in the chaise lounge beneath the silent night the years of sacrifice marched relentlessly across the back of his closed eyelids. He opened his eyes and gazed up into the vast expanse of Mediterranean sky. A trillion stars blinked and twinkled down at him. His children's college years had evaporated into the past. His wife and his colleagues had come and gone at will but Maxwell and his staff had never been allowed to leave Thera.

He felt a tremor in the pit of his stomach and an empty feeling radiated up until it clenched his heart in creeping fear. "*Am I the right person?*" he asked himself once more.

Suddenly one star appeared more brilliant than all the rest. Maxwell fixed his gaze on it. It seemed to rotate displaying several different colors while pulsating rhythmically.

"That's strange," he thought. "My eyes are playing tricks on me." He blinked several times but with each blink the star appeared to get larger, descending down toward him.

His eyes were riveted in fascination as the blinding apparition raced toward him. Just as he felt the overwhelming urge to throw himself from the lounge chair and run it stopped. The object, not large at all, bobbed softly like a balloon halted in mid-air, bouncing gently before his face. He found himself gazing into the most beautiful eyes he had ever seen. The features were fine, the face framed in a brilliant blue light.

All doubt fled from Maxwell's mind as he repeated the familiar words in a hoarse whisper, "Hail Mary full of Grace the Lord is with Thee." Her face floated above him, her lips parted in a gentle affirming smile as he recited the Rosary.

When he finished he deliberately blinked his eyes sure that this figment of his imagination would vanish but when he opened his eyes she was still there. Her smile widened and Maxwell heard a melodious sound that he perceived as laughter. Then she spoke. Her voice was rich and velvety.

"Fear not," she said. "I have come to reassure you of your calling. The Day of the Lord is at hand. Many are called. Few are chosen. You, my son, are chosen. When the fullness of time shall come I shall stand with you and all the world shall bow in devotion to my Sacred Heart. I shall be restored to my rightful place."

Overcome with emotion he reached toward her with outstretched arms. Her presence seemed to recede slightly and his heart felt ready to explode in his chest.

Feeling his pain she reassured him once more, "Have no fear, my son. When you need me I shall come to you." Her image began to recede into the blue-black sky until her presence was again no more than a twinkling starry essence.

Some other man may have imagined that he had fallen asleep to dream. Maxwell knew better. He *knew*. The Mother of God had visited him. His heart was so swollen in his chest that it was actually painful. Dawn was lifting in the eastern sky when he slipped quietly back into the bedroom and slid silently back into bed where Marion slept in peaceful oblivion.

CHAPTER 11

Maxwell awoke to the familiar sound of relentless crashing of sea against rocky cliffs. He rolled over to discover that Marion had already gotten up and was gone. He pressed his palm into the place her body had so recently vacated. The sun, seeping through slightly moving sheer curtains painted bazaar pictures on the cold marble floor.

"Did I dream all that?" he thought. "No," the peace he felt was too real for that. He debated about telling Marion. If she had been in the bed beside him he might have decided to share the vision.

So called "Mary Worship" had been abandoned years earlier when the ecumenical movement had joined the protestant and catholic churches into one Christian organization. Jeff had briefed Maxwell on future plans to unite the religious world even further when Muslims, Jews, and Christians would eventually unite and become known as the Church in Unity. However, on this secluded little island the Virgin Mary still found a place in Maxwell's heart. He was committed to stand in his place on World Day and *she* had promised to be with him: a revelation that he decided he would hide in his heart.

He got up and slowly began to dress.

Max and Leslie were due to arrive for the weekend. The weather promised to be spectacular: balmy and clear. Maxwell was anxious to see the children. They each led very busy lives and it had been several weeks since they were last at Villa Rose.

He found Marion in the kitchen with Stan planning the weekly menu.

"Good morning, darling," Marion said brightly, kissing him on the cheek. "Sleep well?"

"Yes, I did. I feel great, as a matter of fact."

"Stan, I think I'll have my breakfast on the veranda this morning. The air is so crisp and fresh."

"That's an excellent idea, sir. Will you be joining him, madam," he asked, turning to Marion.

"Yes, I think I will. Thank you, Stan."

After breakfast Maxwell joined Rolph in the cavern where the work day routinely began. Rolph had already received the latest report on the crisis in the Middle East where the Confederation of Arab States and Israel were on the brink of an all out war. The United States of Europe had diligently monitored the situation from the onset, pulling appropriate strings to ensure the success of their own agenda.

"I have a tricom ready gentlemen," CC informed them.

George and Rolph took their seats. The consoles projected the images of George and Paul at their respective stations.

"What's going on out there, George?" Maxwell asked.

"Paul can give you a more up-to-date report. Have you got it, Paul?"

"Right in front of me. Do you want a projection or a hard copy?"

"Both," Maxwell said. "I think that would be simpler."

CC whirred softly as the information was received from the Beast. In seconds each man had the information in hand and was prepared to continue the briefing.

"As you can see," Paul said, "the situation is deteriorating fast. Russian war ships are on the way to the Mediterranean. The U.S. has warned them to back off. One more little nudge should be enough."

"It's time to detonate." George said flatly.

"That will do the trick," Maxwell agreed, "but can we be sure we can control the aftermath?"

"Nothing is certain," George said. "The Dome has to go. Take care of it, Paul."

Paul turned to the Beast and typed in a few numbers and symbols. It's done," he said in a tone of finality.

Almost immediately at the ISA headquarters in Jerusalem a coded message came through on a Novastar receiver. Within minutes a team of three men left the building and headed toward the Mosque. It was noon and the Shrine was filled with praying Muslems.

The men concluded the tricom and the room fell silent. Maxwell jumped when the in-house phone rang sharply. Marion's voice was shrill with panic. "Maxwell. Something dreadful has happened. Terrorists have just demolished the Dome of the Rock in Jerusalem!"

She was literally shaking with fear when Maxwell arrived upstairs in the media room. Marion knew enough about the situation to know that repercussions would be severe. Terrorist attacks had been a common occurrence in almost every nation of the world and war was a constant threat. Where it finally erupted was just a matter of semantics, the Middle East being the most likely location.

Maxwell sat down and put his arm around his frightened wife. "How bad is it?" he asked.

They watched together as the newscaster related the tragedy in graphic detail. Hundreds had died on their faces, prone bodies a macabre pointer toward Mecca. Those closer to exits were blown to bits. Marion wept, overcome with compassion as tormented survivors wailed their grief in a great crescendoing lament. Maxwell's composure was shaken. Had he actually taken part in such a ghastly decision? If Marion ever discovered his involvement she would never forgive him. Could he forgive himself?

The United States of Europe was in control of the game now. The die had been cast. The playing pieces were on the board. The Russians holding back the Arab world by the scrap of the neck and the United States desperately trying to keep Israel under control were suddenly moved into uncompromising positions. The stage was set.

Who, how, and when retaliation would come were the only questions to be answered. The whole world held a corporate breath.

An alert from CC brought Maxwell to his feet. "Darling, I've got to go back to the Cavern. Will you be all right?"

"I'll be okay. You go." She let her hand slide from his. "Maxwell," she asked, "will you try to contact Leslie and Max?"

"I planned to do that as soon as I can," he assured her. "I'll be back soon. Please try to stay calm."

Rolph looked worried. "Things are heating up too fast," he said. Muslems all over the world are screaming for blood and many of them are taking it. Look at these reports from Brussels and Mount Weather."

Maxwell looked at the monitors; live pictures from all over the world filled the screens.

"New York/Synagogue bombed-Brussels/Temple destroyed-Jerusalem a death trap. Those are just a few of the headlines," said Rolph.

"I'm getting a code six," CC advised, her voice calm and measured, never betraying any emotion. She was, after all, only a machine.

A code six conference was of the highest security and could only be conducted when the computer in Greece, Belgium, and the United States were synchronized with a triple six code; no communication could transpire without it.

"Russian warships are moving into position. It is our understanding that they are intent on cleaning up in the Holy Land," George stated.

"Is the United States ready to play ball?" Paul asked.

"That is our information."

"What if they don't?" Maxwell asked.

"In that case, the Commissioners are prepared to instigate," George answered. "Pray God it won't come to that," he added softly.

The two super powers snapped and growled circling like two mad dogs, never actually making contact. Enough blood had been spilled by the enraged Arab world to temporarily quench their thirst for revenge as the world tottered on a fragile peace.

Max and Leslie had arrived the day after the attack on the Dome. They were safe. The four of them took comfort, as people all over the world did, in the bond that held them together. They were a family.

On Sunday a rumor was launched that Russia had invaded Israel but the tactic failed to bring about a confrontation and only served to plunge the nations of the world further into fear. The United States of Europe would have to instigate after all.

Chapter 12

A week later the Hurst family were peacefully sharing a late breakfast on the veranda catching up on the world news, a striking contrast to families around the world who lived in dread of being sucked into a nuclear holocaust. Maxwell knew steps were being taken to prevent that from happening, at least prematurely. Such crucial events could never be left to chance. For years a small coalition of powerful men in the United States of Europe had anticipated the need to deliberately ignite an explosive fuse while at the same time guaranteeing the prevention of a full-scale outbreak of nuclear war; and if the naked truth of the plot had been revealed to him from the beginning, Maxwell would not have accepted it. Now even the limited knowledge he had isolated him from his family. They were part of the worried world and he was part of the salvation of the same world, but what a price. He longed to tell them, especially Marion.

"Dad, look at this." Leslie passed the newspaper to her father. "Isn't this interesting?"

A picture of a graph accompanied the story. "Students at Salem High Predict Future" the heading read. Maxwell looked at the picture and handed the paper back to Leslie. "Read it", he said. It was their custom to read and discuss current events each morning.

Leslie began to read out loud. "A group of high school students in New Salem, Georgia, USA claim that the Bible foretells current events in striking detail. Bible experts explain that many of the events outlined on what they call a Visiograph have ongoing and continuous revelations such as the increased occurrence of floods, famines, earthquakes and other natural disasters.

Scientists concur that while it is true that these instances have been increasing at an alarming rate it does not prove the involvement of a 'higher power'. More specific predictions concerning the rebuilding of Solomon's Temple on the ancient historic sight seemed unlikely until last week when the Dome of the Rock was destroyed in a terrorist attack.

There are also predictions about a super world government centered in two human figures—one political and one spiritual. This new government will have its base in Jerusalem and control will be maintained through strong economic sanctions against anyone who refuses to receive some sort of number embedded in his or her hand or forehead. The final conflict comes when the 'higher power' clashes with the powers that be and mankind is saved from total destruction. It is certainly note-worthy that the realignment of Israel's borders last year were accomplished exactly as predicted in the Bible."

What was interesting to Leslie was downright disturbing to Maxwell. He wanted to see a complete copy of this so-called Visiograph. "How can these predicted events line up so closely with our plans?" he thought. He intended to find out. It would do little good to research the Bible. Even if he could find one at Villa Rose he wouldn't know where to find anything in it. "Jeff will know," he thought.

"What about separation of church and state?" Max asked. "I thought there was a law against teaching religion in public schools."

"Let me finish." Leslie read on, "Question was raised as to the legality of such activity on public property even though the principal had given his consent. Mr. Miller, the club's counselor pointed out that the Bible was in the library alongside the writings of Nostradamus, Plato, Muhammad, and the Koran. Students have always been free to quote from any of these philosophical works."

Maxwell drained his coffee cup. "May I have the paper, Leslie," he asked. He tucked the paper under his arm excusing himself, rather abruptly, and left the room.

"What's up with Dad?" Max asked.

"Maybe something in the paper upset him," Marion said. " He has been quite preoccupied lately. I'll have a talk with him later."

Rolph was working when Maxwell arrived in the Cavern. "Have a look at this, Rolph; what do you make of it?"

Rolph read the article and handed it back to Maxwell. "Sounds like someone is looking over our shoulder," he said.

"That's what I thought. Let's do a code six and confer with the others."

CC put them in touch with Brussels and Mount Weather. "Paul is out, but George is ready," CC purred. Do you want me to complete the Tricom?"

"Yes."

"Good morning Maxwell. What's up?"

"George, have you seen a news article about a Visiograph that appeared in a U.S. daily? I believe it originated from a small town in Georgia. New Salem?"

"As a matter of fact I have a copy of it right in front of me. Uncanny how "right on" those kids are."

"Do you think we have a leak?"

"Nah. I've had the predictions analyzed by experts. People who know about these things tell me that the Bible does seem to predict some of these events. Of course they have no idea about our plans and how closely the hammer is hitting the head. I did talk to Jeff and he told me not to worry about it. He explained that the Bible is not meant to be interpreted literally. There are still a few die hards that believe in some foggy supernatural salvation. Pity we can't tell them from whence cometh their help," George laughed. It won't be some far away God who rescues them in the end."

"Does that answer your question, Maxwell?"

"Yes. Could you transfer the information?"

"Sure. Coming over. Oh, by the way, the date for instigation has been set."

"When?"

"Sorry old friend but this is even too top secret for you. Keep your family on the Island for a while though. We are going to secure you down there for a few days."

Maxwell found it hard to believe that they were actually going to perpetrate a nuclear exchange between the United States and Russia in order to instigate an altercation. He had been informed that it was necessary and he also knew that they would do whatever was necessary to keep their plans on target. The two super powers were to be pitted against each other so that the United States of Europe could move in for the kill.

When Maxwell rejoined the family they were still lingering over coffee, engaged in amiable conversation. His mood was gloomier than ever.

"Dad, we were just telling Mom that we need to go back to Paris tomorrow. Max has another interview."

"I'm sorry but that is out of the question. You will have to change your plans. Something has come up and we are all going to stay put for a few days."

"What do you mean?" Leslie demanded.

"Just what I said. You'll stay here."

"That's crazy, Dad! Everything is arranged," Leslie exclaimed.

Marion looked at her husband. He was dead serious. She, of all people, knew how resolute he could be.

"But Dad! I have an interview," Max protested.

"Forget it!" he snapped.

They knew him well enough to know that the sight of his back as he left the room was the end of the matter.

"What in god's name has gotten into him?" Max demanded.

"I don't know but I intend to find out," Marion said, as she hurried out after Maxwell.

He was just leaving the path to the beach when she caught up with him. "Slow down, darling. I'm winded."

She linked her arm in his and he pulled her along beside him. He was walking fast and purposeful. He didn't seem to notice that she had to trot at an uncomfortable pace to keep up with him. On and on he walked until the beach gave way to treacherous, craggy cliffs impossible to climb. They had come to a dead end. Maxwell sat down on the damp sand and Marion fell exhausted beside him. He pulled his knees to his chest, cradled his head on his arms and wept.

"Maxwell!" Marion said, in alarm. "What is it?" She had never seen him in such a state. She reached out to hold him. He clasped her to himself as desperately as a drowning man clutches a life preserver. Suddenly he was kissing her in a way he had never done before, bruising her lips. Then he rolled her over in the sand. The violent pounding of the surf echoed in his veins as he became insane with the sound of it. He didn't hear Marion as she cried out in pain as he took her. Then it was over. He rolled face down in the sand and his body was wracked with great wrenching sobs of shameful relief. Marion, herself bruised and battered, pulled him into her arms and cradled him like a baby. All the fear and uncertainty drained from him and seemed to soak into the wet sand. He was going to be okay. But he still could not share anything with Marion even now but he no longer felt alone. Like the Eternal Virgin, Marion would always be there for him. He gently brushed the sand from her face and kissed her bruised lips softly.

"Forgive me," he moaned, "Marion, I'm so sorry. Forgive me."

CHAPTER 13

Leslie sulked for the rest of the day but little by little Maxwell was able to woo her into a more civil state of mind. Leslie was not exactly spoiled, but she was very independent and accustomed to having her own way most of the time. Max, on the other hand, usually managed to take things in stride and had made arrangements for a later appointment. By midweek everything seemed to be back to normal.

The Hurst family was having lunch outside. A cool breeze added to the sparkle of the day. The weather was perfect the sea lapping lazily at the rocky shoreline. The birds chirping wildly in the olive grove.

"Those birds sure sound wound up today," Marion commented.

"Sure do," Leslie laughed, "they sound like the Mormon Tabernacle Choir singing off key."

"They *are* noisy alright," Maxwell agreed, lowering his paper.

The sea was exceptionally calm, almost too calm, lending a slight uneasiness to the otherwise peaceful scene, a scene that was about to be violently shattered and permanently altered.

A distant sound, above the din of the birds, came roiling toward the Island. The roar, like rolling thunder, could be felt as well as heard and was getting louder and louder like the sound of an approaching freight train.

"What's that sound?" Marion asked.

Max got up and went to the railing at the edge of the veranda. He cocked his head to one side. He scanned the hazy horizon. What looked like a giant sea monster was slithering wildly toward them. Surely his eyes were playing tricks on him. "What in God's name *is* that?" he muttered to himself.

At the same moment shouts came from the garden. It was Joseph running toward them with his spade pointing out to sea.

Almost as though on key, Rolph appeared with the news. "Tidal wave! Coming this way."

"Look!" Max shouted.

A white wall of churning water surged toward them.

"Everybody! To the Cavern," Maxwell commanded, overturning his chair in his haste. He herded them toward the elevator where they were joined by the household staff. They would be safe in the Cavern.

The staff had never been allowed to enter the Cavern. It was another world to them. CC commanded the very center of the huge computer complex surrounded by an array of sophisticated technology. Shiny sterile surfaces and soft twinkling lights gave the room an eerie atmosphere.

Maxwell led them into the conference room and from there to the lounge where they huddled together in fear. The lights flickered and went out.

"Dad, the floor is pitching," Leslie screamed in terror.

Martha began to pray loudly in her controlled English accent and Carmen began to cry unabashedly. The rocking sensation lasted only a few seconds before the emergency generator kicked in and the lights flickered back on.

"How long do we have to stay down here? Marion asked.

"It'll be a while," Rolph replied.

"Anybody else need a brandy?" Maxwell asked as he went to the liquor cabinet. "We may as well try to relax."

The brandy definitely helped. Carmen who never drank became silly and came down with a case of contagious laughter easing the tension as the time passed.

"I think we can go have a look now," Maxwell announced. "Rolph, you come with me."

"Dad, let me go too."

"All right son, but the rest of you stay put until we give you the all clear."

The three of them headed toward the stairs. The elevator would be useless with the diminished power. Max was in the lead and reached the top first. He pushed against the door.

"Uh oh. The door won't open, Dad."

Maxwell pushed hard against it, "It's stuck all right."

The three men combined their strength and pushed the door. Inch by inch it slowly opened. A thick layer of wet sand had packed against the bottom of the door. They stepped out into the glaring light.

"My god!" Rolph gasped.

The great wave had crashed into the Villa with devastating force. The windows were all blown out and what was left of the furniture was heaped in shapeless debris. The basic structure was still standing amid glass and sand everywhere. The yacht and the hovercraft were both missing. The gardens were ruined: the roses gone. It was deathly silent. Even the birds had disappeared.

Maxwell dreaded the thought of summoning the household, but he knew that the sooner they faced this crisis, the better they would be able to handle it. "Go down and get the others, son," Maxwell said. "Tell them to expect the worst."

The frightened little group trouped up the stairs. One by one they emerged. Carmen was crying again as she picked up broken pieces of precious artifacts. Stan hurried to the kitchen and pantry area to survey the damage. Not much was left but they had plenty of stores in the Cavern. Three of the rear downstairs guest rooms were fairly well intact. They would have a dry place to sleep and food to last until supplies could be brought from the mainland.

Martha found enough brooms, mops and other cleaning supplies to put them all to work. The Hurst family worked as hard as the others earning even more admiration and respect from the staff.

Sometime later Maxwell and Rolph left and went back to the Cavern.

"CC get me a Code Six," Maxwell demanded.

CC began to comply, "I'm sorry Maxwell, but I am unable to connect a Code Six."

"What the hell does that mean?"

"I can get you Brussels."

"All right. Get me Brussels."

"Paul! What in Sam hill is going on out there? We were just hit by a tremendous tidal wave. Villa Rose is nearly destroyed. We have no transportation. The Sea Witch and the hovercraft are both gone. CC claims she can't connect a code six."

"That's because the Russians just bombed the hell out of Washington!"

"They *what*?"

"We instigated, Maxwell. We underestimated their capabilities. We just didn't anticipate a full retaliation on the part of Russia. They took out five U. S. cities. It's pandemonium over there."

"Oh my god!"

Maxwell and Rolph stood slack jawed in disbelief as Paul related how the incident had been instigated by an almost simultaneous discharge from inside Central Command at Cheyenne Mountain in the United States and Tyuratam Space Center deep within Russian territory. Russia took out Washington, New York, Los Angeles, Atlanta, and Miami. The U.S. got Moscow and Saint Petersburg.

"We couldn't stop it in time. Now it looks like the earth itself is in rebellion. We have seismic activity convulsing the planet!"

The impossible had happened. The nations of the world had gone through stage after stage of nuclear disarmament since the United Kingdom had spearheaded the movement back in 1958. Strategy had flip flopped back and forth over the years from mutual assured destruction, to city busting where millions of innocent people could be held hostages in mega cities and back again to counterforce where only military targets were destroyed.

When the United States of Europe was born, they took their place as *the* Super Power and immediately took the responsibility of holding Russia, China, and the United States, as well as the rest of the world in check. Many old concepts had been resurrected like escalation control and damage limitation. Disarmament took on new meaning when not only the number of warheads was restricted but their size as well. Anything over three megatons was illegal. The bombs themselves were vastly different from their predecessors. The discovery of cold fusion had triggered the development of earth penetrating weapons that detonated beneath the earth's surface creating shock waves that literally shook the target down with little or no radiation involved. The test's that had been conducted did little to prepare the world for the chaos that mother earth was experiencing now as she thrashed in the throes of agony with earth rending seizures coming as regularly as a woman's birth pangs.

"The United States is temporarily crippled without Command Control Three," Paul said. "We are trying our damndest to restore communications with Mount Weather and as soon as we do we will get a Code Six and connect you."

"What can we do?" Maxwell asked.

"Nothing. Just sit tight. We have disaster relief in place. Our Crisis Control Centers are manned—We were prepared. We will just have to create more tent cities than we planned and provide more food but we *are* prepared."

Without a Code Six further dialog was useless, so the conference was terminated. The two men sat long moments in silence. This could be the end of it all. A slight rolling motion sent them plummeting toward the stairs. How could they explain to the others what was happening in the world?

"Would they even believe such catastrophe was taking place?" Maxwell thought. The floor pitched beneath him violently. They would believe him.

CHAPTER 14

It took three days to get a Code Six. In the meantime they worked feverishly getting the Villa back into some semblance of order. Hard work proved to be a blessing creating an antidote for the worry that consumed them. Each of them had someone out in the battered world that they were concerned about. Maxwell had gently told them of the destruction and if it had not been for the continual after shocks that rocked their little island they probably would not have believed such a disaster had actually happened. Maxwell resisted telling them the whole truth and it was for their own peace of mind that they were kept uninformed.

Rolph and Maxwell hurried to the Cavern to answer an alert from CC. "I have a Code Six for you, Maxwell," she said gently, alive with animation.

"Ah, this is what we have been waiting for. Thank you CC."

Rolph had already taken his place at the console and was ready to receive. The image of George and Paul filled the screen as the tricom was completed. Maxwell was immensely relieved to see George. There had been no way of confirming his safety until now.

"George! So you really are okay?"

"I was here at Mount Weather when D.C. blew. There is no way to describe the devastation, Maxwell. We never imagined they would get off five! One for one, that's what we were guaranteed."

"The 'State of the World Report' from the U S of Europe is coming over," Paul said. "You need to study it thoroughly."

Maxwell described the rolling motion they were experiencing and how the sea kept taking huge bites out of the beach, coming dangerously close to the Villa.

"That's mild compared to what's happening here," George said. "We've lost half of California **and** Florida to the sea.

"Good god," Maxwell breathed.

"Yes. The quake on the west coast was so severe that a strip of land fifty miles wide and stretching from Mexico to Oregon was literally wiped off the map. When that happened the ocean level was raised worldwide. The coastlines are permanently altered. Florida had to be evacuated because virtually the whole state is submerged under three to four feet of water. It's flooding as far as South Georgia where huge sink holes are appearing, swallowing up everything in sight and creating deep spring fed lakes."

George was silent for a moment before he went on. "There is just no way to describe how I felt when we flew over those areas to assess the damage. Great smoldering heaps stand where there used to be cities. We sure as hell didn't mean for it to go this far!"

Maxwell felt a sick feeling creeping up from the pit of his being, resulting in a visible tremor. "What about the death toll?" he asked, dreading the answer. "What about Jeff? And Mikeal?" During the long years of isolation his friends had become as precious to him as his own family.

Mikeal appeared beside Paul on the screen. "I'm fine Maxwell, as you can see."

"Me too!" chimed in Jeff from Mount Weather.

"Thank god! You guys *are* all right. Damn but I'm glad to see you!" Although Maxwell was overjoyed at seeing his friends he could tell that George was anxious to get back to business. "Uh, George. What about the death toll? Are casualty lists available yet?"

"Partial lists are coming in. We know the numbers are in the millions but our main concern now is getting the survivors settled into Crisis Control Camps," George explained. "We are dealing with major earthquakes every day, somewhere around the globe. The worst is in the United States. The continent is in perpetual motion. It sure is a hell of a feeling!"

"This certainly *is* more than we bargained for," Paul said, "but then, it *is* working out to our advantage."

"That's right," George agreed. "The temporary confinement of most of the world's population lends itself very well to our plans. We are revising our system so that citizens will be required to receive their personal identification number before they leave a Crisis Camp."

"That's the Lomalaser that implants the chip?"

"Yes. The number is actually burned into the skin but is a painless process and is invisible until scanned."

"It will be possible to account for every person over the age of twelve in every nation on the planet," Paul added. "Isn't that fascinating?"

"It's a little hard to believe that people will go along with all that," Maxwell mused.

"Why shouldn't they? It will be for their welfare. When the new system begins people will be falling over themselves to comply! That's how the thing is set up. They already see us as their life raft-we are their salvation, in fact."

"If they don't comply they don't eat. It's that simple," Paul added in a matter-of-fact tone. "Oh I suppose some of them will end up in Confinement Centers but it will be of their own making if they do. We aren't going to incarcerate them **and** feed them but we **will** incarcerate them—well at least until they come to their senses and get with the program."

"That's right. As soon as they agree to co-operate, they will be allowed to leave." George had masterminded this system himself and it was engineered for success from the start.

"If I may change the subject," Paul said, grinning with pleasure. "Maxwell, we have some super news for you. You are coming out to Brussels within the next few days. We have a place prepared for you and it is time that you met the Commissioners."

"I'm coming out?" Maxwell asked, his pulse quickening. "For good? The family?"

"Yes, the whole family. Phase II is complete. Congratulations!"

Maxwell thought only of Marion. He wanted to tell her—share her excitement.

"We'll have a grand reunion," Jeff promised. "It'll be great to get together again."

"Yes and don't forget to bring my wife," teased Mikeal.

"Hopefully we will have Command Three restored by the end of the week," Paul said. "We'll send a hovercraft for you then."

The conference ended but not the briefing. Rolph and Maxwell were obligated to thoroughly review the 'State of the World' report. Communication was still down except for Novastar. They were anxious to get this bit of news and would stay in the Cavern until every depressing detail had been digested. The assault on Mother Nature had the world spinning. The only consolation that could be had was in the fact that a nuclear winter was not part of the scenario as scientists had proclaimed for years. Over the years they had banned and perfected the bomb but the devastation had been horrendous just the same.

When Maxwell finally left to go and join Marion his step was slow and deliberate. They were going out into the world, yes, but what kind of a world awaited them? When at last he found Marion he took the mop from her hand, pulled the bandana from her hair and held her close. Silent minutes slipped away. Then he told her. *Everything.*

Chapter 15

Marion, Maxwell, Leslie, and Max prepared to leave Thera. Rolph would stay behind and maintain CC. The Villa was to be restored and would continue to serve the Commissioners for future private meetings.

The restoration of Command Three and the tricom coincided with the arrival of the hovercraft. They were in a dither to leave but Maxwell regretted having to say good-bye to Rolph and he knew there would never be another cook like Stan. But just the thought of seeing some green wide-open spaces was a source of pure joy. He'd had enough of rocks and water to last a lifetime.

There wasn't much to pack. Nearly everything they owned had been washed away with the tidal wave. Marion and Leslie were looking forward to new wardrobes. Clothes were not a priority for Maxwell or Max but they *would* have to be properly attired.

Maxwell found himself looking down with some nostalgia as the hovercraft spun silently up and away from Thera, the only light in a sea of darkness. Villa Rose got smaller and smaller until it seemed engulfed by the relentless brooding sea.

The hovercraft was soon landing at the Athens International Airport where they were to transfer, under the cover of night, to a private jet that would take them on to Brussels. Within minutes they were airborne again. The flight was uneventful. Marion dozed contentedly in the seat next to Maxwell. Max snored softly in his recliner and Leslie curled up comfortably on a plush sofa and browsed through a fashion magazine.

Maxwell was unable to sleep. He sat very still. His eyes were closed and his hands were folded in his lap. He had a curious stirring in the back of his brain; his thoughts were making unconnected flight paths through his mind. In spite of the fact that he had been in on much of the ground work for this whole affair many things seemed to still be 'out there somewhere' and he wasn't quite able to pull it all together. He wasn't even sure that he hadn't made a first class ass of himself for allowing them to cloak his existence for all these years. In fact, he may have thrown in the towel long ago if it hadn't been for the vision. The vision was both awesome and humbling. No matter what **they** had planned *he* knew in his heart his life was destined to fulfill a divine purpose. This was the comfort to which he always fled as he did now.

Dawn was beginning to break as the jet came thundering down over the sleeping city of Brussels. Maxwell was dazzled by the beauty of the ancient city with its many gilded church spires with brightly colored steep pitched roofs. The sunlight danced and glistened as it bounced off the many faceted buildings that were the jewels of Brussels. Several old castles complete with moat, turrets, and formal gardens could be seen surrounding the city.

"Marion. Wake up. We are flying over the city." He shook her gently. Leslie, who had fallen asleep woke up too and the three of them gazed down at what looked like a picture out of a fairy tale.

Max woke up last. "What's that down there?" he asked, pointing to rows and rows of Quonset Huts doting the landscape. "Is that part of the city?"

"No." Maxwell laughed. "We've left the city. We are approaching the airport. Those are hot houses you see down there."

"As in a greenhouse. For flowers?" Marion asked.

"No. It's the way grapes are cultivated here. And most other fruits and vegetables too. But Belgian grapes are known worldwide."

"And just how do you know all that?"

Stan told me. Stan taught me everything I know about food. He was a walking encyclopedia when it came to food and he only imported the best for our use on Thera."

"I've read that the food here in Belgium is fit for royalty," Leslie commented. She was the well-traveled connoisseur of the Hurst family.

"I'll be satisfied if it's just fit for consumption," Max mumbled, thinking of the rations of the last few weeks at Villa Rose. Max was hungry—hungry in more ways than one. He was hungry because it was morning and his body chemistry told him that it was time to eat. He was hungry to get on with his life, if that were going to be possible. He had some things that he wanted to discuss with his father and he promised himself that he would do so at the earliest opportunity.

Somehow the weariness of their past ordeal had robbed them of any spark that life had held. It seemed as though life, as they knew it, had ended. The newscasts on Thera had been demoralizing, leaving them with a hopeless void that had not been filled with anything other than a test pattern and a high frequency tone.

Now as the four of them looked down at this lovely little country with its many peaceful villages and farms, lush green rolling hills, and slow moving canals and rivers: each felt a stirring of hope. All was not lost after all. They were landing smoothly and safely at the Brussels National Airport.

CHAPTER 16

A long, shiny black limousine was waiting on the runway. Two men stood beside it. The shorter of the two was obviously the chauffeur. The taller one strode out to meet them smiling with pleasure.

"Welcome to Brussels!" Paul grasped Maxwell's hand in a firm grip before turning to Marion, Leslie, and Max, whom he greeted with equal warmth. "My god! It's good to see you people." He pulled the women into the circle of his arms before herding them all to the waiting limo.

They chattered merrily as the limo sped down a wide tree-lined boulevard. The sun was still low in the eastern sky and created luminous lacy silhouettes in the huge old trees. The road wound its way through miles of gently rolling countryside past neat bungalows and compact farms.

The hour passed quickly for Paul and Leslie who engaged in lively conversation concerning the latest fashions and where they could be obtained. Paul seemed very well versed in the subject and Leslie was more than anxious to get on with life in a decent wardrobe. The car entered a graveled country lane at the bottom of a steep hill twisting and turning until it reached a steel gate with a guardhouse on either side of the lane. Extending in both directions from each guardhouse was a high fence that enclosed the entire estate. The guard seeing the official flags on the limo opened the gates and waved them on.

The limo continued up the hill winding back and forth until it emerged at the very top.

Marion could not contain herself. "Oh, Maxwell! Are we in heaven?"

Before them stood a castle so beautiful it was nearly indescribable.

Maxwell laughed and pulled her closer so he could whisper in her ear, "It's our very own Camelot, darling."

The limo moved through the wide-open gate in the stonewall that surrounded the castle and stopped in the courtyard outside the main entrance. The castle was tucked away amid a forest of tall virgin timber making it so private that it was nearly undetectable except by air. The living quarters were built into the turrets leaving plenty of space for conferences, balls, and dinner parties fit for royalty. The formal gardens were the most unusual in the world; the topiartry work outstanding and imaginative. Strolling there promised to be a repetitive and enjoyable affair.

Paul helped Marion out of the limo holding her hand gently. "Welcome to Gasbeek, my lady," he said gallantly. She curtsied demurely and did not release his hand immediately. As they walked he lectured them much like a tour guide. "This castle was built in the 15th century by the Duke of Eldenburg. It was donated in 1912 to the State and was used as a museum until recent years when it was acquisitioned by the United States of Europe for an official residence and conference center. It will be your residence now, at least temporarily."

"Wow! This is really something," Max said with open mouth admiration.

"Ah, yes," Paul agreed, "but you must be famished. Come. This way. Breakfast is waiting." He led them down a stone path and around a privacy hedge into another part of the garden where a table laden with food stood amid beds of brightly colored flowers. They all sat together at one large glass topped table while two men in spotless white uniforms and white gloves stood by ready to serve them.

"Go ahead, Marion," Paul urged, "try the salmon. It's delicious."

They were served what seemed to be an endless array of fruits, meats, and breads of every shape and kind imaginable served with the richest butter and spreads available. Milk, juice, and coffee were poured from silver carafes.

"Good-bye good figure," Leslie lamented brandishing a croissant covered with strawberries and sweetened whipped cream. Their conversation was centered on food making it easy to pretend that they were here for an extended European holiday. For the moment there was nothing more important than breakfast in the garden.

After the eating binge came to an end, Marion asked Paul to give them a tour of the castle. She was very impatient to see their new 'home'.

"Come on, darling," she said, pulling her husband out of his chair.

Maxwell got up wearily. He longed to sleep. "Tell you what. I'll tour with you as far as our private quarters. There the tour ends for me. I'm beat."

"We'll start at the top then," Paul said cheerfully. "Want to walk up or take the elevator?"

Paul grinned as Maxwell shot him a disgusting look. He led them through glass doors into the formal dining area with its thick glass walls that had the elusion of bringing the garden inside. Marion caressed the smooth wood on one of the graceful chairs. She was picturing herself entertaining in this elegant setting. A smile played at the corner of her lips. A massive stone fireplace separated the dining room from the half-moon foyer where one could choose a healthy climb via the spiral staircase or a quick trip in the elevator.

"The main living quarters are in this turret," Paul explained. "It is the tallest and strongest of the towers. Of course, there are other interesting areas to explore, such as the ballroom and the conference area. The communications center will really impress you, Maxwell. The computer in there is something else." Paul noticed Max's eyes light up and then he remembered how Rolph had instilled a lifelong fascination in the young man. "Of course you will have free access too, Max," he added warmly.

Paul pushed the elevator button and the doors slid silently open. They stepped in and were taken swiftly to the third floor. Stepping out into the dimly lit foyer was like stepping into another world. The wall circling around to the master-suite was resplendent with paintings done by masters such as Rembrandt, VanDyck, and Raphael. The paintings displayed under perfect lighting would have rivaled the most elaborate art museum.

"Round here and your home," Paul gestured. He opened a door and they entered a huge room flooded with morning sunlight.

"Mom!" This is awesome!" Leslie exclaimed as she threw herself in the middle of the huge round bed. It was situated in the center of the curve with a desk and bookshelves built into either side of the bed. Windows filled the space above allowing sky and sunlight to fill the room.

"Man, just look at that view!" Max said. The countryside rolled out before them like a huge quiet and serene pastoral painting, stretching as far as the eye could see.

Opposite the bed was another fireplace exactly like the one in the dining room and in the guest suite on the second floor. Maxwell sank back into one of two oversized easy chairs. "Imagine us here, Marion, in front of a roaring fire. Snow pelting the world outside. Cozy, huh?"

"Mom, come look at this garden tub," Leslie called from the next room. "We could all take a bath together!"

Paul didn't follow them into the more private part of their rooms but waited politely while they explored. Curiosity got the better of him when he heard hysterical laughter coming from the bathroom and he peeked in to discover all four Hursts sitting in the empty garden tub fully clothed. "Room for one more?" he asked, sheepishly.

When it was time to look further Marion suddenly decided that she would rather stay with Maxwell. The tub was more than she could resist and a nap before lunch would be so refreshing. "Go along without me," she urged. "I'm going to stay with Dad."

"Yah. I need someone to scrub my back," he teased.

Paul winked at Maxwell and Marion turned crimson. The children laughed.

"Oh, by the way," Paul said as an afterthought, "when you get hungry ring down and have something sent up by way of the silent butler. When we finish our tour I intend to take these two into the city for a shopping spree and lunch." He linked his arm in Leslie's who was beaming her approval.

"That is if you can find time to eat," he said with a teasing smile while escorting the young people from the room.

So the President and his lady spent the first morning at Gasbeek in luxurious, lazy lovemaking that would prove to be memorable private hours not often repeated. Maxwell was on the brink of revelation to a panic stricken world and Marion would have to be content to give him up to his calling.

As for the children, Paul had already introduced Leslie to a world of opulence at once intriguing and irresistible, almost as intriguing as Paul found the young Leslie to be. Max, on the other hand, would soon be so involved in the mechanics of the new world system that he would have little time for anything else.

Chapter 17

Marion gave the elegant dining hall one final inspection. The fresh cut arrangements were exquisite. The tables were impeccably set with the finest china and silver arranged to accommodate the ten Commissioners and their wives along with George Middleton, Paul Roberts, Jeff Richards, Mikeal Aristotle, and the Hurst family. The lady of Gasbeek was being capitulated into elite society with a swiftness that left her breathless. In spite of this Marion carried herself with an air of confidence that was inbred and she anticipated with pleasure each minute of the up coming events.

She and Maxwell dressed with deliberate leisure aware that every precise movement was as perfect as a well-orchestrated symphony. When they finished they stood side by side before a full-length mirror for a final inspection. Maxwell reached for Marion's hand. The image they saw was one of absolute beauty—a prince and his princess. They each stared at the other. Locked within this image neither dared to breathe their thoughts; instead they turned and embraced each other carefully.

Max, Leslie, and Paul were already in the dining room when Maxwell and Marion arrived. Leslie, who looked stunning herself, was taken with the beauty of her parents as they entered. "Oh!" she exclaimed. "Mom, Dad, you look absolutely—regal!"

Marion laughed as Leslie embraced her. Paul stood at Leslie's side. He was handsome and charming. Marion instinctively felt his influence in her daughter's life. "Leslie is in love with him," she thought. "My god! He is at least twenty-five years older than her!"

Marion was haunted by memories of Paul's attentiveness during the long lonely years of Maxwell's voluntary exile. Mikeal, surrogate though he was, was seldom around. It was Paul who was there to see to her needs when she, by necessity, was separated from Maxwell for extended periods. A slight shaft of jealousy pierced her heart which she immediately dismissed as she returned her daughter's embrace.

Jeff, Mikeal, and George arrived early. The intimate group of friends gathered together in one room for the first time in years and the laughter, backslapping, hugs and tears were enough to create the atmosphere of a circus. These men held a special place in the heart of the Hurst family. Jeff was a spiritual ally, Mikeal had been especially good to the children, Paul had made Marion's sacrifice bearable, and George managed to maintain a very delicate balance that had kept them all on course for the past twenty years.

This private reunion seemed all too short when it was announced that the commissioners and their wives had arrived. They each took their place to dutifully receive them.

"Anya," Marion said warmly as she took the hand of the German Commissioner's wife. "What a lovely name."

"For a lovely lady." Maxwell offered while he effortlessly moved the woman from Marion's sphere to his own. The Commissioner beamed proudly as his plump middle-aged wife blushed beneath the praise. They, as the others, were completely taken by the charm of this American couple.

Dinner was a bazarre affair. The size of the party encouraged intimate simultaneous conversations and although the participants all spoke English the varied inflections intoned sounded more like a symphony of singing blackbirds.

Commissioner Slavitt and his wife were seated with the Hursts, George, and Paul. "Your daughter is very lovely," Anya said to Marion. Leslie, animated and radiant, sat directly across from them at the large round table. She was talking intimately to Paul who was listening intently as though they were the only two people in the room.

"Thank you, Anya. At the moment I believe she is very much aware of it herself." The two women smiled knowingly.

"I have a daughter also. She is married and has a child."

"So. You are a grandmother. Congratulations."

Anya beamed proudly as she talked of her beautiful little five-year-old granddaughter.

"Will there be a grandson?" Marion asked.

A slight look of pain crossed the older woman's face. "There was a grandson," she said sadly. "He was killed in a freak accident. Of course since they had their quota, my daughter had been sterilized. So now-no. No grandson."

Marion looked at her daughter then at her son Max. She had indeed been fortunate. Would she be fortunate enough to become a grandmother? She looked at Paul and Leslie. Her thoughts appalled her but before she could return her attention to the woman at her side Paul looked up and caught her staring at them. He smiled.

Later as they mingled in the garden over coffee and liqueur Leslie approached her parents. "Guess what? Uncle Mike has invited Max, Paul, and me to accompany him to the Riviera this weekend." Although phrased as a statement there remained a slight suggestion of a question in Leslie's voice.

Maxwell, surfacing from a deep discussion of the economy with the French Commissioner grinned at her indulgently. "Wonderful!" he said, nodding his consent. He returned to his previous conversation failing to notice or receive Marion's disapproving look.

"Whatever were you thinking of, Maxwell?" Marion demanded while pulling the comforter from their huge round bed. "Can't you see what is happening to your own daughter?"

"What's happening to our daughter?" Maxwell asked alarmed.

"She's falling in love. That's what's happening. Right under our nose!" Marion, obviously perturbed, stood with her hands on her hips, her lips set in a worried frown.

A huge relieved grin spread across Maxwell's face. "Who," he demanded, "is the lucky man?"

"The lucky man, you big blind lug, is your dear friend, Paul!"

"Paul! Paul?" His voice held an incredible unbelieving question mark. "You gotta be kidding!" He slapped a palm across his forehead. "God in heaven! And I've just given her permission to go to the Riviera with him! What in hell are we going to do now? Paul is one of our dearest friends." Maxwell's face darkened, then he said, "That bastard! He better keep his hands off my little girl!"

Now Marion was alarmed by her husband's reaction. "I don't think any harm has been done. Yet..," she muttered under her breath.

"I'm going to excuse myself from the ladies tour tomorrow. Leslie and I are going to spend some time together."

Maxwell looked up gratefully. "Can you handle it, darling? There is no way I can be available tomorrow. The Commissioners are meeting all day."

"I'll handle it," she assured him. If only he knew how many times throughout the years she had *handled it*. Her heart wrenched at the memories of how involved Paul had been in helping her to do just that. She wondered how much help he would be now.

Chapter 18

"**A**ctually the Russians have played right into our hands." George was addressing the Commissioners assembled in the meeting room adjacent to the Command Center at Gasbeek. "We didn't intend for the destruction to be as extensive as it was or the repercussions so severe but now that it's done, well, let's just grab hold of the ring."

He picked up the slim blue book on the table and held it high. It was a copy of the WORD. Smiling ruefully he said, as though toasting an occasion, "To the global community, gentlemen."

In spontaneous response each held his copy aloft resounding, "To the global community and the WORD!"

Maxwell and Jeff had been introduced to the Commissioners socially the evening before but this was the first official meeting and the two were impressed with the informality and camaraderie of the group. They seemed more like a fraternal order than what they actually were: *rulers of the world.*

"We are prepared to implement section five-article six." George announced. "Our Lomalaser Identification System and Tracker known as LIST are ready to implant. Mobile units equipped with the lasers will be installed at exit points in each Crisis Control Camp. No one will be allowed to leave without his or her number."

"When will that be?" asked the French Commissioner.

"Just as soon as it is safe to return them to their own homes," George replied.

"It is getting harder and harder to retain my people when they feel it is unnecessary," the German Commissioner added.

"This is true, comrade, and we understand. We will be and *are* prepared to begin as early as next week, especially in Sectors where it is safe. It may take longer in the United States and Russia of course, considering the destruction in those two countries."

"Perhaps they will be more appreciative of our recovery efforts. It may even make for a smoother transition to the global community," Paul added.

Maxwell Hurst and Jeff Richards had been approved by the Commissioners to head the Global Community. Now it was time to prepare the citizenship of the world for transition to the new system.

"Today at six o'clock we will begin to unravel the world's greatest mystery. Prepare to emerge from your cocoon, Maxwell. We are about to celebrate your coming-out party!" George said standing to his feet. The others stood as well and for the size of the admiring group the applause was thunderous.

A button was pushed to receive the latest *state of the world* report before adjourning for lunch. The huge screen covering one wall of the conference room sprung to life giving them the latest stats on world conditions, recovery efforts, news, and weather around the globe. Whatever news was breaking around the planet appeared here first. Information was fairly repetitive of the last report except for a bit of information that appeared for the first time. It was a report from the Hubble Space Station. The telescope had picked up some unusual information. It seemed that several bright objects were detected in the seventh quadrant at the edge of the seventh galaxy. They appeared to be moving rapidly toward the earth's galaxy. This could not be confirmed. At least not yet.

The bizarre news created a mild form of diversion within their ranks. "What do you think, Comrades? Should we send this item out to the camps?" George asked.

The only form of communication that the people throughout the world had was a nightly news release broadcast to each Crisis Control Camp through electronic bulletin boards.

"I say we should," Paul answered. "It may spark some interest and break the monotony."

Everyone agreed and the news was broadcast. Little did they realize that before the day was spent the objects would have entered earth's galaxy and be picked up by a NASA airborne observatory. The objects were destined to create much more than a mild diversion as they moved in what appeared to be precision formation toward the earth. The proposed peace plan and the news of the Commissioners meeting in Brussels were nearly dwarfed by the UFO story.

That evening in the privacy of their quarters Marion told Maxwell about her day with Leslie. "She would not accept any of my arguments questioning the wisdom of encouraging a relationship with Paul. She called my position on the subject ridiculous and irrational."

"I'll be the first to admit that our daughter is strong willed and determined, but she *is* a good girl and she *is* an adult," Maxwell added.

"What are you saying? We should just stand by and let this happen?"

"Of course not but she does have the right to make her own decisions."

"She intends to go off with him this weekend!"

"Do you want me to have a talk with Paul?" Maxwell frowned at the thought, but he knew he would have to try and avoid any friction on this issue.

"Maxwell, would you? Please? I think that would help. At least maybe you can determine if this is just an infatuation on her part or if she is being encouraged."

"Would you like a little diversion?" Maxwell asked glancing at his watch.

Marion shrugged when he flicked on the TV. "More statistics on recovery? How intriguing," she said flatly.

"No. Come here. I think you might find this interesting.

The life size image of a handsome, impeccably dressed, newscaster looked out at them in his usual impersonal way.

"Heads of State from every nation began gathering today in Brussels where the United States of Europe is working out the final details of a plan for peace. This plan will be unveiled within a matter of days. Meanwhile tremendous effort is being put forth in assisting the Red Cross to alleviate the crisis caused by the recent altercation between the United States and Russia. Seismic activity seems to be diminishing slightly. Rescue efforts continue and the death toll now stands at four million."

His voice lowered and took on a grave tone. "Partial casualty lists of those who perished in the stricken cities in the United States and Russia have been updated. As usual these lists will be posted on the electronic bulletin board located in the public information area of your camp."

"Here is an interesting bit of news," he said with slightly more interest. "Astronomers at observatories around the world have been tracking mysterious pulsating lights in the heavens. They appear to be approaching our galaxy at a tremendous rate of speed. These photographs taken from aboard a sky born observatory reveal that the objects are moving in a precise formation toward our planet. Dr. Gerald Kuper, aboard the Skylifter, says that if the objects continue to travel at the same rate of speed they will soon be discernable with the naked eye. He says that they should be entering our atmosphere soon, possibly within the next twenty-four hours."

Leslie and Max burst into the room even before their parents had time to discuss the phenomena.

"Jeez, Dad. Did you see those things out there? What do you make of it?" Max demanded.

"Beats me," Maxwell said. "They must be traveling at a tremendous speed because when I saw the first report this afternoon those things were way the hell and gone beyond our galaxy! I'd better get back with George."

At the same moment the phone rang. It was George.

"Yes we are watching. All right. I'll be right there." Maxwell hung up the phone. "Come on, Max, let's get over to the complex. Something's up. They have a NASA briefing on line."

As it happened the concern over Leslie's infatuation with Paul was dwarfed by the events of the next few days. The trip to the Riviera was cancelled but that failed to cancel the feelings that were mounting between them. The intensity of the situation proved, instead, to be a catalyst.

Chapter 19

Maxwell and his son hurried into the computer complex just as a communication was being received from NASA. The Commissioners were already assembled.

"Looks like we are in for a little excitement," George said to Maxwell. "It looks like an army of those things are descending on us! If they continue at their present rate of descent and direction we are on a collision course."

"We haven't got an inkling about what may be going on," Paul added. "No intelligence exists on a sighting of this magnitude. It only adds data to a file already bulging with UFO information."

"We are on the highest military alert but there just isn't anything else we can do except watch and wait," George said.

Their attention was drawn back to the monitor where another live report was assimilating from NASA. A high-ranking officer addressed them in a boring monotone, "It is our opinion here at NASA that the objects we are observing are intelligence controlled. So far they appear *not* to be a military threat. All attempts at communication have failed. However, we are continuing our efforts to make contact. We will keep you updated with continuous visual surveillance along with regular and timely oral reports."

The giant monitor was suddenly filled with the spectacular sight of the descending objects in all their brilliance.

By the following afternoon the UFOs, sighted barely thirty-six hours earlier, appeared to be hurling down on earth. The Commissioners and the others, along with panic-stricken people in camps around the world, could be classified as the crooked and stiff-necked generation as they kept a constant vigilant watch on the heavens. The great brilliant balls of fire became steadily more visible even in bright sunlight.

While George, Paul, and Maxwell were obligated to observe the phenomena from the Computer Center with the Commissioners, Marion, Leslie, and Max had set up their own private observatory beneath the clear Belgian sky on a hillside just outside the castle wall. They relaxed in comfy garden chairs and munched on an endless variety of picnic foods from laden baskets. Late in the afternoon Mikeal and Jeff joined them on the grassy knoll and they settled in for some serious stargazing.

The unknown objects appeared to be getting larger as they came hurling toward earth.

"They are going to hit us," Leslie stated with finality. "My life is over before it begins!" She thought of Paul and the gentle kiss they had shared as he left her in the garden the night before. Paul was the most wonderful, kind person she had ever known. Leslie realized at this moment that she had loved him since childhood.

By mid morning they had moved to recline on blankets spread on the soft ground and now Leslie and Marion lay together staring up into the clear blue sky and beyond at the advancing Orbs. Marion pulled a forbidden icon from beneath her blouse where it secretly rested between her breasts and began to pray in a hushed whisper, "Holy Mary Mother of God."

Leslie was saying her own prayers and as if in answer Paul knelt beside her and pulled her from her mother's side. Maxwell arrived moments later and Marion's attention was diverted from Leslie and Paul to her own distraught husband who settled down between mother and son, placing one strong arm around each of them.

"There was not one damn thing we could do inside," Maxwell said, looking down into his wife's grateful face. "We can wait out here just as well," he said, looking up into the cloudless sky.

"Holy Mother of God!" he exclaimed. The spectacle was much more awesome in real life. Their brilliance rivaled the sun in all its glory. They appeared huge as they continued to descend slowly. Rows of flashing lights circling the objects pulsated in sequence like colorful flashes of lightening.

On the other side of the world in the Western Hemisphere the sightings created pandemonium and fear as the many faceted diamond like spheres hovered over the earth like great birds of prey in a pitch-black sky.

It seemed as though humanity held a corporate breath, helpless in the face of shared dread. Minutes seemed like hours.

"Look!" Max croaked, "Something's moving. Those things *are* being controlled," he said swallowing hard.

"Shit!" Mikeal said falling back. "Something is coming out!" He jumped to his feet and literally ran from the scene.

"Look at that!" Maxwell exclaimed as the underside of the orb directly above seemed to fall away revealing a huge amber chamber of some sort.

Suddenly it was totally dark and fear gripped them in common dread as three lightening-fast saucer-shaped craft shot out from the chamber in three different directions. Maneuvering silently they zipped back and forth above the darkened countryside covering huge distances in seconds while creating mesmerizing light displays of every color in the rainbow. They were glistening and intensely white. Each time one of the craft banked sharply what looked like a human form could be seen under a crystal clear dome on the top. The three ships came together high above the castle as though performing a delicate ballet, then divided and descended slowly in three different directions until one was hovering directly over Gasbeek in the sight of everyone for miles around.

Marion literally jumped into Maxwell's arms when a loud voice like clapping thunder broke the breathless silence.

"Fear God and give glory to Him; for the hour of His judgment has come: Worship Him who made heaven and earth and the sea and the fountains of waters."

Before anyone could move or speak the first ship had sliced off to the side and was replaced by a second and a loud voice cried, "Babylon is fallen, is fallen, that great city, because she made all nations drink of the wine of the wrath of her fornication."

That ship also whirred off in a blur of light and was replaced by a third and again a message thundered across the heavens, "If any man worships the beast and his image and receives his mark in his forehead or in his hand the same shall drink of the wine of the wrath of God, which is poured out without mixture into the cup of His indignation; and he shall be tormented with fire and brimstone in the presence of the holy angels and in the presence of the Lamb. And the smoke of their torment ascends up for ever and ever; and they have no rest day or night whoever worships the beast and his image and whoever receives the mark of his name."

"Sons of men!" Boomed a voice in a deafening command. "Be patient. You are called to endure to the end! Keep the commandments of God the Father and the Faith of Jesus His Son!"

Once again they were presented with a dazzling display of intricate maneuvering before each disappeared into the great amber vault in the underside of the waiting orb. The huge sphere began to move slowly away into the waiting sky. Suddenly with lightning speed they were gone-just a few of many stars twinkling in the far reaches of the universe.

Chapter 20

No one had a clue as to where the unidentified flying objects had come from or where they had gone to but by the following afternoon it was confirmed that the strange message they had brought to the inhabitants of the earth was straight out of a Bible. Bibles had gradually lost influence during the New Age of Enlightenment and Pluralism. Of course there were die-hard Bible believers in every country and oddly enough the most resilient proved to be in Russia. When Communism had fallen at the feet of democracy, the Russian people had embraced a simple Christian faith and were converted by the millions. Similar phenomena had occurred in China.

The meeting in Brussels the next day was top secret. "Are you familiar with these sayings from the Bible?" George asked Jeff.

"Not really," Jeff confessed, "but I found them here in Revelation, Chapter Fourteen. It seems to be the exact message we heard from those ships." He flipped open a black book to a red bookmark. "I read it years ago when I was in Seminary, but Revelation was written for first century Jews who were suffering persecution at the hands of the Roman Empire. It certainly doesn't have any relevance for our time."

"What about the report from New Salem in the United States?"

"I recall that," Maxwell said. "That incident was in the paper a few months ago. Some kids and their predictions about the future."

"It seems they got their predictions from a Bible," George said fingering the black book that lay open before them on the table. "They were interrogated again at a Control Center this morning. They deny having anything to do with the UFO incident. They say we were visited by angels and continue to babble some gloom and doom nonsense."

"It is obvious this elaborately staged hoax is an attempt to thwart our plans," George stated. "The only nation other than the United States that has the technology to pull off something like this is Russia."

"Rudoski wouldn't be behind it," Paul said. "He has fully cooperated with the system."

"Yes, but he knows about the Lomalaser. If I recall, he did have some doubts."

"Nah, it has to be coming from the Christian sector," Jeff said, rubbing his forehead thoughtfully. "They are the only segment of society that would oppose our plan for peace."

"Well," George said, "at this stage of the game it doesn't matter who in hell orchestrated it. What we have to do now is convince our people that it *was* orchestrated!"

"That shouldn't be too hard," Paul offered. "We'll just leak a few details of our own top secret files. Perhaps something from segment 51 in Nevada. Give them a glimpse of how far Star Wars has actually progressed."

There was some debate among the Commissioners about the wisdom of leaking information from the Nevada test site; some felt it would be more effective if the information came from Europe.

"People are still experiencing the effects of what happened between Russia and the United States," Paul argued. "They will be more apt to listen if we pin it on one of them."

In the end they voted to target Russia as the perpetrator of the most spectacular hoax of the century. They, after all, had both the motive and the technology.

"Get over to the Beast, Paul," George said. "Get a code six and pull this thing together. I want a report on the six o'clock news."

"You got it." Paul headed for the elevator that took him to the basement where he was transported under the busy boulevard to the Berlaymont building and nerve center for the Beast.

George turned his attention back to the Commissioners. "Gentlemen," he said, "It is time to move on before the populace recovers from this bit of excitement. We must hit them with a still bigger shock." George looked straight at Maxwell. "Stand up my man. Your time has come!" He bowed in symbolic homage.

Maxwell sucked in his breath and swallowed hard. All eyes were on him. He knew what George was alluding to. How well he knew. The stage had been set. His debut planned and his success assured. So why was his gut in a knot? Why did he feel like he had to excuse himself and escape to the men's room?

"I felt like a perfect ass," Maxwell told Marion who was curled up under his arm as they sat on a comfortable sofa waiting for the evening news to begin. "I guess they were expecting me to get up and utter something profound, and I had to excuse myself and shoot off to the men's room!"

"Darling, anyone can get a case of the nerves. You've been anticipating this for years. It's easy for me to understand how you must have felt," she laughed. "Probably just like I felt when Max was born. Nine long months of waiting while he was being formed inside me could never prepare me for the actual moment of birth. Maxwell, my dear, you are about to be born!"

Just moments before the telecast began, Max, Leslie, and Paul joined them in their private quarters. Paul and Leslie were fast becoming a twosome and considering the magnitude of recent events that fact was becoming less and less of an issue with Leslie's parents.

"An investigation is underway concerning the spectacular hoax perpetrated last night by dissidents in the Soviet Union. In an attempt to undermine the Peace efforts on the part of the United States of Europe, Christian factions in opposition to global unity confessed responsibility for staging the most elaborate technical ruse in history. Their efforts aimed at derailing the peace movement have failed."

The newscaster promised more updates before announcing the unveiling of the peace plan that was scheduled for the following evening.

CHAPTER 21

George had just left. He and Maxwell had gone over their speeches for the last time. It was a go; no backing out now. The big question the world was asking was about to be answered.

Would they swallow the hook? Maxwell was sick with apprehension. Marion turned the water on in the garden tub and began to fill it with steaming water. Their attire was carefully chosen and laid out. The four of them would be presented together at the close of Maxwell's speech. His reincarnation would soon be realized.

"Come, darling," she said, "bathe with me." She took his hand and gently pulled him toward the dressing room.

He followed obediently allowing her to help him undress. Marion slipped off her only clothing, a white satin robe, and they both stepped into the warm swirling water of the hot tub. The tension flowed out of him as he began to relax under her soothing caresses.

The Hurst family was driven to the Berlaymont where the live broadcast would take place. People all around the world were gathered in Internet Information Centers or Crisis Control Camps waiting with anticipation for the message that was destined to reach them all.

The opulent Judicial Chamber was unusually hushed although the galleys were filled with dignitaries and their guests. The Council of Ministers and the Commissioners sat with Maxwell at the semi-circular conference tables situated on the main floor facing the stage.

Marion, Max, and Leslie waited behind thick velvet theater curtains with George.

The well-known figure of George Middleton, man of the world, emerged from behind the curtain and approached the podium. He allowed for polite applause before he placed a hand on either side of the ornate lectern and looked down at the Commissioners and then up at the galley. A slight knowing smile played at the corner of his mouth as he began.

"Ladies and gentlemen of this court and citizens of the world, it was announced yesterday that a World Peace Plan was ready for unveiling. The frightening and awesome events of the past days and weeks have made it mandatory that complete and immediate control be taken by intelligent and peace-loving people on behalf of the populations of this planet. No one nation can be trusted to maintain peace and insure justice and equality for *all* men. The United States of Europe has long maintained a goal of global peace and prosperity for all the peoples of the earth. It has, in fact, been the very salvation of our tottering civilization in this volatile and critical period of our world's history.

If we are to survive we must have a common goal. That goal must be to work together to rebuild the stricken cities in Russia and the United States, to create jobs for the unemployed, and to produce enough food to feed a hungry world. We must structure a peaceful and non-violent society in which mankind can at last realize the utopian dream of peace on earth good, will to *all* men. A society in which we no longer seek our own good but rather the common good of ourselves *and* our brothers."

He paused for a moment his piercing blue eyes holding them as a captive breathless audience. Then he said, "In order to accomplish this goal of a united world we have appointed from among us a representative to serve and lead us. A man who will stand at the helm of our new world government and guide us into our destined glorious future." George's voice became deep and intimate as he leaned toward them. He continued in an almost pleading voice, "I beg you to understand what I am about to reveal to you."

He paused again. "Just suppose you had a tool that was precision made for a single specific job. You would save that tool until it's time of usefulness arrives." He paused a third time emphasizing the importance of his carefully chosen words. "The man I am about to present is like that tool! He has long been loved and respected in many nations by multitudes of people. He is the man for *this* perilous hour of our greatest need. It is my highest privilege to present to you the first President of the United States of the World!"

Maxwell slowly pulled himself up from his seat. His broad shoulders, the tilt of his head, and his purposeful stride seemed vaguely familiar to those who watched him as he walked slowly toward the steps that led to the podium. George moved out to meet him and the two men embraced.

"Congratulations Mr. President." George stepped back and said, "Ladies and Gentlemen, honored guests, allow me to present President Maxwell Hurst."

Maxwell faced the waiting populations of the world. The reaction was immediate and diverse. Some began to weep. Others gasped in open-mouthed amazement. Others simply fell back in a dead faint as they recognized Maxwell. Standing alive before them was a man they had mourned for nearly twenty years. A president assassinated at the height of his popularity by the bullet of a madman. Maxwell stood silent, still incredibly handsome despite his age, a slight smile playing at the corners of his mouth as he waited for them to regain their composure. He ran his hand unconsciously through the thick gray hair over his left ear smoothing the wiry strands that hid a scar where the bullet had carved a line across his skull.

The twelve Ministers rose from their seats clapping softly in respect. The twenty four Commissioners followed and then the galleys erupted in shouts and whistles of approval. A few just sat as though dumb struck. At the same moment thunderous shock waves of recognition were reverberating throughout the world.

Maxwell raised his arms. The chamber fell instantly hushed at his command for silence. His voice broke with emotion as he spoke. "Thank you," he began. He felt a new power flood his whole being as he gazed out at these adoring people.

He raised his arms again, this time in victory as he addressed them in a tone that thundered in every corner of the globe. "My fellow citizens!

Salvation has come to our world! Peace *is* a reality! Prosperity *is* a certainty!" Wild enthusiasm again filled the hall as the crowd voiced their approval. He lowered his arms and again a hush fell.

"I realize," he continued, "how difficult it is for you to understand what is happening. I personally beg your forgiveness for seeming to deceive you. Please believe me when I tell you that the extreme measures that were taken were absolutely necessary to overcome the evil advances of the godless societies in our world. Believe me also when I tell you that these years have been extremely difficult for my family and me. We have a motto that has encouraged us through the years and in closing I would like to share it with you. It goes like this: 'May I have the courage to change the things I can, the serenity to accept the things I cannot change, and the wisdom to know the difference.' All of us here at Central Control pledge to keep you well informed on the peaceful and hopefully smooth transition to our new system of government."

At that point, Marion, Max, and Leslie joined him on the stage and the first family of the United States of the World stood arm in arm, smiling broadly as they accepted the adoration and approval of the cheering audience. Moments passed, then Maxwell bowed slightly, waved farewell, and they disappeared behind the velvet curtain.

Chapter 22

A small coming-out party in Maxwell's honor followed the broadcast. Those few masterminds who had generated and nurtured his gestation attended it.

The garden at Gasbeek glowed in the soft light of well-placed gas torches, creating ghostly dancing figures as the light flickered on fanciful carved shrubbery.

"Rolph! What a wonderful surprise!" Maxwell embraced his old friend and companion. "This is great. How have you been? I didn't know you were coming over."

"This is one event I wouldn't have wanted to see on the net," Rolph laughed. "Marion, you look radiant as always," he said taking her hand and pressing his lips against it.

"Rolph, you are such a dear. Thank you for coming."

Paul, Leslie, and Max arrived together. Leslie noticed her mother and father talking to a tall man in a black suit across the garden. Something in the way he stood seemed familiar to her. He turned his head slightly and she recognized Rolph immediately. "Uncle Rolph," she called out affectionately as she hurried to fling herself into his open arms.

Rolph swung her around like a child and then he put her down and turned to hug Max. "You both look great!" Belgium seems to agree with you although I can't help but notice you are both in need of a tan," he teased.

"Paul! You old son of a gun." The two men greeted each other warmly. Leslie linked her arm in Paul's and the older man eyed them suspiciously.

"Well, now," Marion chimed in. "Isn't this turning out to be a fine reunion?"

She felt strong arms encircle her waist from behind, "not without me," a familiar voice said.

"Mikeal!" she squealed with delight as she turned in his arms to face him. "My old flame."

Maxwell extracted his wife from Mikeal's arms, feigning mock jealousy. "The flame just went out, old boy. How are you doing?"

As the two conversed George arrived with Jeff. "Here Here," he called out, "don't start the party yet."

"How could anything start without you and Jeff?" Maxwell laughed. "Didn't you mastermind this whole damn thing?"

"That's right," Jeff said, "and now we're singing 'got the whole world in my hands, got the whole wide world in my hands, got the whole world in my hands.'" Jeff sang it like an old Negro spiritual and got everyone's hearty approval.

When dinner was over the men excused themselves and convened over coffee in a secluded part of the garden.

"I wonder how many momentous and life-changing events are planned in a quiet garden?" Maxwell mused out loud.

"More than you would care to know about," George said finishing his brandy and picking up a copy of the WORD. He held it up for all to see. "This is it. This is the beginning and the end. This is all she wrote! Our success depends on this book. How it is presented, how it is accepted and how it is enforced."

"We are all set," Jeff assured them. "Joint meetings are scheduled to introduce the WORD to each Ecumenical Branch. I don't see a problem. Narrowing them down to three philosophies was the hard part. Whittling three down to one will be a breeze."

"How do you figure that?" Maxwell asked.

"Easy. All three Branches believe in God. All three claim Abraham as their founder, and all three have unity as a goal. Easy," Jeff said again, snapping his fingers. "It's the rebellious fanatics in each Branch that will give us trouble."

"Those who rebel will be responsible for their own good fortune," George added. "It's all right here in the WORD. Obedience is the *only* choice!"

"By this time next week we'll know where they stand," Rolph said. "If they agree with our plan they won't object to the coding system we have planned."

"That's right and by this time tomorrow night they will know where **we** stand." Paul said, referring to Jeff's debut.

"May I propose a toast?" Mikeal offered. He stood and lifted his goblet toward Maxwell. "To our President! And to our Bishop!" he added turning to acknowledge Jeff.

"To our President and to our Bishop!" they all chorused.

"Incidentally Maxwell, here is a copy of your speech. You need to look it over."

"I've written my own speech, George. I'll let *you* look it over." Maxwell's firm, matter-of-fact tone astonished them and at once all eyes were on him. "Well I *am* the President am I not?" he grinned. What seemed like a joke was a turning point in Maxwell's life.

"How about you, Jeff?" I suppose you have written your own speech, too?"

"Yes, I have George," Jeff said smiling. "Would you like to read it?"

"You're damn right I would," George growled.

Aware that their business had come to an end and desiring to part as friends, Maxwell pushed back his chair and prepared to leave. "Gentlemen! Goodnight. I hate to leave such good company but I believe my wife needs me." He grinned sheepishly and they all laughed as they got up to leave. The strange surge of power that he had felt earlier was back and now as he approached their suite he had the overwhelming urge to share it with Marion. She was asleep in their huge round bed. Moonlight flooded the room and he could make out every detail of her naked form beneath smooth satin sheets. He undressed and carefully slipped into bed beside her. His presence stirred her and she moved close to him. Aroused by her nearness Maxwell exerted his newfound cosmic power and Marion was overwhelmed.

Chapter 23

Maxwell, George, and Jeff met in the breakfast room the next morning. George had a stack of printouts. "Here are the reactions from your speech last night. This is just a sampling from around the world," he said picking up the first one. "This is from a Camp in India. The survivors there accept what is happening to them as part of a divine plan for their lives. 'We accept the reincarnation of President Hurst as our leader'."

"Listen to this one from South America, 'The people in this camp are ecstatic. Maxwel Hurst has long been considered a saint in this region of the world,'" Jeff read. "And listen to this one from Russia, 'The people here are shocked at the immensity of such a conspiracy. Where will it all lead they ask?'"

"This one is similar," George continued, "Crisis Control Camp #4380 in Wisconsin reports: 'The people here admit they have always believed there was some kind of conspiracy involving President Hurst's assassination. They are shocked to find out the truth but at the same time they feel confident that they can trust him.'"

"Did you get one from Georgia, USA? The camp where those kids have been causing such a stir?" Maxwell asked.

"I think I saw one in here somewhere," George said while sorting through, looking for that particular report. "Here it is, 'Crisis Control Camp #7520, New Salem, Georgia, USA: the occupants of this camp have been influenced by publicity involving a small group of radical Christians who have opposed pluralism and global unity since it's inception. They warn that President Hurst could be the embodiment of an evil entity predicted to rule the world. They are a small faction, however, and do not reflect the views of the Ecumenical Branch. The majority of the citizens in this camp accept the transition."

"Hey. Whoa!" Maxwell protested. "An evil entity?"

"That's a bunch of crock," Jeff shrugged. "Those ultra conservative Christians are always spouting off some kind of garbage. Consider the source!"

As a whole the reports were very encouraging and Maxwell began to relax even more. His confidence in himself was growing, along with a strange magnetism that even he was not yet aware of. His appearance with Jeff that night would seal his fate.

"Good morning," Leslie announced herself cheerfully, "I hope I am not interrupting anything." She kissed her father and picked up a thick piece of cinnamon toast laden with creamy butter.

"Of course not, darling. Come join us," Maxwell said, clearing the table of the reports.

"Leslie, you look radiant this morning! Sleep well?"

"Yes, thank you, Uncle George. Wasn't it a wonderful party? Just like a family reunion for Max and me."

"In a way it was," Jeff reflected. "Re-united with all the people who meant the most to you and Max during your growing up years."

"Daddy, Uncle Rolph has invited me to come to Thera for a holiday. He says I need to get away from these Belgian calories and get a sun tan." She placed a hand on her hip smoothing the slight roundness. "Stan can tailor a diet for me. Oh, it will be *so* wonderful to see the staff again!"

"That will be a nice break for you, dear. Rolph isn't leaving today? No, of course not he will wait until after the broadcast tonight," he said answering his own question.

"He is leaving tomorrow," Leslie said, "and Daddy, Paul is going, too."

"What?" Maxwell began to protest.

"I'm sending him," George explained. "He is going to work with Rolph finishing up the laser codes. Everything must be in place by this time next week. In fact it might be a good idea to send Max too. He is a whiz when it comes to CC."

"Excellent idea. He can keep an eye on his sister!" Maxwell laughed with some resignation.

"Well, I'd better be off," Jeff said getting up, "I am meeting with the Minister of the Word this morning. We need to go over a few things before tonight. See ya'll later."

They didn't see Jeff again until that night. Maxwell worked on his speech while George conferred with Rolph and Paul. Max and Leslie packed while Marion and Mikeal spent the afternoon enjoying their reunion.

That evening everyone was again found at the Berlaymont. It felt like a repeat performance, only this time the booming voice of the announcer minced no words as it went out to people gathered around internet screens in camps around the world. "Ladies and gentlemen. Please welcome the President of the United States of the World. Maxwell Hurst!"

Maxwell came striding out, head erect, shoulders back a striking image of self-assurance. "Good evening," he greeted them in a warm confiding tone. "The third phase of our Peace Plan is about to be unveiled to you tonight. You can be confident that within days we will have you safely back in your own homes and life will get back to normal. However for many of you what was normal will never be the same again. We express our deepest sympathy for those who lost loved ones in the recent events of the past few weeks. We do have good news to share tonight. Our goal is to guarantee that all the peoples of this great planet enjoy the basic necessities of life. We promise you that your children will no longer go to bed cold or hungry. Starvation will be a thing of the past. Kindness and humanity will be the hallmark of our government. Fairness and justice our standard."

All this was possible and Maxwell felt the power come up in him as his promises crescendoed. "Just as we are one government, we will, from this time forward worship one god! We will be known as the people of the WORD."

Maxwell held up a small blue book, a book that would become familiar to them in the days and months ahead. "Leading us in this phase of the plan the commissioners have elected a man you all know, love, and respect. This man has become a legend in his own time as he has fought to bring about a peaceful, fair, and just society in all nations. Because of this one man's efforts great strides have been made in areas of civil rights and economic fairness among the poorest and most oppressed nations of the world. Please welcome theologian, statesman, beloved citizen of the world, and Administrator of the WORD, Bishop Jefferson Brandon Richards."

Maxwell stepped forward to welcome the renownd black leader. "Congratulations, Jeff," Maxwell said as the two men embraced. President Hurst smiled broadly as he surrendered the podium to his tall handsome friend.

Jeff, calm as he seemed, was visually shaken with the emotion of the event. He waited patiently for the thunderous applause to subside. "What a joyous occasion for me!" He paused to regain his composure and wipe the tears from his face. "To be chosen to serve you in such a capacity is an honor, but to serve with President Hurst is honor beyond measure!" He was truly moved and his mood was contagious.

"Many of you have heard me preach. Relax! You will be happy to hear that this will probably be the shortest sermon of my entire career!" He waited for the laughter to end. "You will soon realize that we are a government of few words and much action!

However I do have a word for you this evening. A word that is old and familiar. A word that must, I repeat **must** become a part of your new life-style if we are to survive on this planet. That word dear friends is obedience. The message has always been and will always be the same. *Obedience*!" His voice became emphatic and the seriousness of his tone could not be mis-taken. "I give you a simple equation," he leaned forward on the podium in an intimate pose, pausing before his punch line "Obedience equals blessing. Disobedience equals curse. It is as simple as that."

Standing erect he finished in a more matter of fact tone. "In a few short days you will be leaving the camps to pick up the strands of your lives and get the wheels of our great society rolling again. Our President will lead! We will follow! He is our chosen one! We are his people!" Jeff shouted out this procla-mation and the galleys went wild. He had to calm them in order to continue.

"Before leaving the camps every citizen will be required to receive a personal identification number. These numbers will replace all existing systems. It is of utmost importance that you receive your number. Without it you will not be allowed to carry on any legitimate or legal business. It will be impossible to buy even one slice of stale bread without it!" He paused briefly smiling down at them.

"Don't worry, ladies, the number will not be visible to the naked eye. It is not our intention to disfigure you.

There is much to be done. There is a job for everyone. We must be willing to work together to ensure the success of the system. We *will* succeed! We must trust each other and be obedient to our leaders. No task is too small. No sacrifice too great to ensure peace for all the people of the United States of the World!" He lifted his arms, closed his eyes and pronounced a benediction upon them. "Bless you, my brothers and sisters! God bless each and every one of you!"

Chapter 24

"I've got great news," Maxwell announced with the exuberance of a child. "We are *all* going to Thera!"

"Daddy!" Lesie protested, supposing that her father was going on a watchdog mission.

"Now don't get ticked off, Leslie. As your president I intend to be involved as much as possible," he said giving her a pat on the bottom. "And that doesn't necessarily apply to your love life. Rolph and Paul are going to be up to their ears in work. Max and I can help."

"Take your time and finish your breakfast. I'm going up to help Mom with the packing." He kissed Leslie on the cheek before leaving. "Cheer up. We can all use a holiday." Maxwell was unaware that his voice carried a new commanding tone.

The flight from Brussels to Athens was uneventful. The welcoming throng at the airport was a pleasant surprise and Maxwell found it exhilarating as the adoring crowd pressed in to see and touch him affectionately. Secret Service Agents edged them toward the waiting limousine. Maxwell turned and waved, smiling broadly, before disappearing inside the waiting car. News of the motorcade traveled before them and all along the twisting route from Athens to the Port of Piraeus people gathered to cheer and wave.

"Good things come to those who wait," Maxwell mused remembering his first trip over this same road years earlier.

"Yes," Marion said, smiling up at him. "Perhaps our time *has* come at last."

The short trip to Thera on the Sea Witch was a happy experience, another antithesis to an earlier trip fraught with apprehension. The sea was calm and the sky crystal blue. Maxwell was on top of the world! His family and closest friends surrounded him, the whole world adored him, and life was just beginning. "Rolph, break out the champagne," he said. "Let's celebrate!"

Upon their arrival they were welcomed by the household staff with the warmth and sincerity of a long separated family. Rolph beamed as though he alone was responsible for this touching reunion.

"Come. Come. Come," Martha said herding them into the comfortable sitting room. "Stan has prepared a feast for you, but first, you must relax. Come. Come," she said again as she patted and fluffed the pillows on the huge inviting sofa and chairs that filled the room. Only when she was certain that they were all comfortably seated did she excuse herself to help the others in the meal preparation.

"Rolph, the restoration is fabulous," Marion said looking around. "Really lovely. I want to see the rest of the villa but I am too exhausted at the moment."

"Well I'm not," Leslie announced pulling Paul to his feet. "Let's explore a bit before dinner."

Marion watched them leave. "I should get up and go with them," she thought. "Leslie is forever looking for an opportunity to get Paul off somewhere alone." A frown marred the smooth lines around her mouth as her imagination took command of her senses.

"Let's go downstairs, Dad." Max could hardly wait to see if CC was up and running.

"I'm with you, son. Anyone else care to join us?"

Rolph got up to go. Marion shook her head. She looked at Mikeal who grinned up at Maxwell and said, "*Somebody* has got to keep the first lady company."

"That is no longer your responsibility, Mikeal, and don't you forget it."

"When you are not here darling it is *still* his responsibility," Marion said patting the sofa and inviting Mikeal to sit next to her. "So you better hurry back!"

"Hey, pop. That sounds like a threat!"

Maxwell laughed and put his arm around his son, "Nah. She's my woman, Max."

The elevator dropped them quickly to their destination and the door slid silently open. The caverns held a unique fascination for the three of them. It was here that Maxwell and Rolph spent years working together becoming close allies as they mapped the future. For Max, it was the intrigue of being on the edge of an adventure so exciting that it literally consumed his imagination. They moved almost reverently down the long carpeted corridor.

A soft clicking sound was replaced by a gentle whir as she went faithfully about her duties. Max hurried ahead. "Ah, CC," he thought as he stood before the most magnificent machine man had ever created. He ran his hand over the smooth shiny surface lovingly.

"You can't make love to her, Max," Rolph teased. "She's only a machine after all."

When they laughed CC was activated and her voice was familiar and melodious. "At your command, Rolph," she said sweetly. "Do I detect Maxwell and Max with you?"

"You do indeed."

"Then greetings are in order," she purred.

Maxwell stood silent while the other two men exchanged greetings with CC. He had always felt a little stupid talking to a machine!

"What have you got for us, CC?" Rolph asked. As he pushed keys and pulled levers, screens sprang to life and information was spun out at top speed. He studied the charts thoughtfully. "They need our spare banks," he said. "Several sectors have exceeded the population projection and space is not available in Brussels. No problem. CC can handle the overflow."

"What sectors are we talking about? Maxwell asked curiously.

"The United States," Rolph said tapping a key that called up a map on the wall monitor. The image immediately changed to a view of the Southeastern sector that was partitioned into several regions. "A few taps on the keyboard and I can zero in on any region in the world. Once I locate the region I can secure data on any citizen in that particular region."

"Wow!" Max exclaimed, "Can you give me a demonstration, Uncle Rolph?"

"Not until after next Friday. That's when the system will be activated. At that time we will begin to see how many citizens will go along with the system and receive their registration number and how many we will have to assign to Confinement Centers."

"It looks like you will be staying here indefinitely, Rolph."

"Hey. I don't mind. At least I still have a job and somebody has to keep CC company."

"I'll stay with you, Uncle Rolph," Max offered with a grin. "This is home to me."

"Wouldn't we all like to stay here?" Maxwell thought wistfully. "Just wouldn't we all?"

They arrived upstairs just as dinner was about to be served. Marion and Mikeal were waiting in the dining room but Paul and Leslie hadn't returned. They entered just as the party was about to be seated. Leslie flushed and radiant apologized. "I'm sorry, Mom, no time to change. The sunset was too glorious to miss," she said looking up at Paul with adoring eyes.

"God I could kill him," Marion thought as she remembered some of her own silent sunsets.

CHAPTER 25

"It just doesn't make any sense going to America to register. Why can't we just go back to Brussels? The days at Thera had served to solidify Leslie's feelings for Paul and she was distraught at the thought of separation.

"Because it is the best place for me to begin public exposure," Maxwell explained. "The people there will be the most receptive. Besides I have roots there and I haven't seen my family in years." He picked up his briefcase and turned toward the door to leave. "No more discussion. Your mother and I are ready to leave."

Traveling the globe was becoming a way of life for the Hurst family. All connections went smoothly and before long they were settled in on a private jet headed for the United States of America.

Maxwell relaxed in an overstuffed leather recliner, eyes closed, hands folded in his lap. "I can hardly believe that in a few hours I'll be back in America. A life time away!" The thought excited him although at the same time he was appalled by the changes that the short war had exacted on the country.

He would also soon be able to assess firsthand a society that he had helped to shape over the years. Such changes as socialized medicine, collective farming, federalized school systems, ecumenical religious centers, and mega markets that narrowed down competition had inevitably prepared the citizens for the new order and were all part of the plan.

Maxwell opened his eyes and looked out at the clear night sky. Stars twinkled and blinked across the heavens. The memory of another night not long ago haunted him. George and the others had convinced him, as well as the rest of the world, that the UFO thing had been a hoax to sabotage the plans for a united world. Not all nations were completely sold on the idea of giving their allegiance to the United States of the World. Some still doubted although they didn't have a choice in the matter. The part about the code was what bothered Maxwell. But then that was the most sensible part of the plan the ultimate credit card! "If the plan is going to be foiled it will be foiled on this one point", he thought. "I've got to demonstrate my confidence in the system. That's the reason we are going to Bangor for a public registration." Satisfied with himself, he dozed off into fitful sleep.

"Mr. President, we are on the ground," the flight attendant said in a gentle voice. Marion was already collecting her things but Max and Leslie were still asleep.

"We're here! Wake up!" Maxwell didn't even try to hide the excitement in his voice. He felt like a kid at Christmas. They had landed at Dullus International Airport but they wouldn't be heading for Washington because it didn't exist anymore. Instead they boarded a hovercraft and left the deserted airport and headed toward Mount Weather in Virginia. Memories came flooding back.

Nothing seemed even vaguely familiar to Leslie or Max until they entered the parking garage. The huge concrete vault sparked some remembrance in Leslie, but it was the elevator ride down to the bottom of the complex that brought a smile to them both.

George met them in the lobby and took them to his suite. He had living quarters in the complex and his office was next door.

"Well, this is cozy," Marion commented, looking around at the well appointed living space.

"It's comfortable," agreed George. "It gets a little close at times."

"I'll bet it does. Where do you plan to stash us?"

"Oh, we have a penthouse for you, Mr. President."

"Great. That's settled. What about my schedule? What's the agenda?"

"Well, that's tight too. We have arranged for you to view the damage in several sectors. That's for tomorrow. We also have you scheduled to make a special appearance in Atlanta, then on to Camp David for a conference. After that, I believe your family is expecting you in Maine for a reunion. Your whole family will report for registration on Thursday morning. That event will be broadcast live before the camps are emptied on Friday." George handed Maxwell a copy of the schedule. "How does that sound?"

"A bit rigorous but challenging," Maxwell said, looking over the material.

Dinner that night was a bit subdued. Jet lag had gotten the best of them. "I believe you'd better show us to the penthouse, George," Maxwell said soon after they had eaten. "We are about done in."

A female officer escorted them to the elevator. The elevator stopped after ascending several floors and the door slid silently open. They stepped out into a garden foyer livid with green plants. The florescent lighting created the closest thing to the great outdoors that could be imitated this far underground. Their quarters were adequate and comfortable. They certainly had privacy and they *most* certainly were safe! The four of them went immediately to their beds and slept like rocks!

The phone was ringing and Maxwell reached groggily for it. "Yes? Okay. Thanks," he said thickly. He hung up, rolled out of bed and pulled on his dressing gown. He walked to Marion's side of the bed and sat down. She was sleeping peacefully. "Honey," he said, shaking her gently, "time to get up."

"Uhmm," she murmured retreating beneath the covers.

"Come on, darling," he said, pulling the covers down.

She opened her eyes sleepily. "What time is it?"

"Seven. We have to be ready to leave by nine."

Marion, Leslie, and Max were scheduled to leave for Maine.

"I'll see you next week," Maxwell promised as they boarded the hovercraft that would take them back to Dullus for a flight to Bar Harbor. He hugged Marion one last time. "Take care of yourself, darling."

"Bye, Dad. See you soon." Max shook hands with his father while Leslie came into his arms for a more affectionate farewell.

Soon after they left, Maxwell's hovercraft departed as well. He had been shown pictures and dvd's of the devastation but nothing could have prepared him for what he saw that day. The penetration bomb that had hit D.C. had left a huge crater where once stood the Capitol and surrounding buildings, including the Smithsonian, White House and everything within a three-mile radius where the bomb had entered the earth. It left a heap of rubble of unbelievable magnitude burying thousands of people in their cars as they had tried to evacuate the city. Now after more than three months the stench was still unbearable.

"My god!" Maxwell breathed.

"As bad as this is, it could have been worse," George said. "With penetration bombs most of the radiation is kept underground, and since the destruction is done by shock waves actually shaking down structures the radius of total destruction is much smaller."

"Is this what the other cities got?"

"They all got the same thing." George pointed out the window. "Notice how abruptly the damage line stops. That's the unique thing about these bombs. There isn't a nuclear storm involved at all, just this tremendous shaking. We've never been able to test more than one at a time, so nobody could have anticipated what five of them at once would do."

"That's what spawned the earthquakes that have occurred since the attacks?"

"That's right. Nature was on our side this time. She played right into our hands."

Flying over undamaged parts of the city reminded Maxwell of a deserted ghost town. Most of the citizens had been assigned to Crisis Camps for their protection. They flew over several of the tent cities surrounding the area but were not scheduled to make a stop.

Flying south over deserted towns and hamlets gave Maxwell an eerie, lonely feeling. Every so often he noticed a flurry of activity on the ground. Fields were being plowed and worked by people who reminded him of ants on an anthill.

The Crisis Corps, civilians housed in Crisis Control Camps, and all citizens involved in any capacity in the food and energy industry made up a temporary work force engaged in recovery work, cleaning up rubble, and supplying necessities to a world not only fractured by the bombs but also by the earthquakes that followed.

The hovercraft landed a few hours later at Metro South International where a limousine waited. Hartsfield had been completely destroyed by the bomb that fell on Fort McPherson. Now, this newer airport looked like a military base. Personnel had been called upon to carry on all necessary functions to keep the basic structures of society intact. The Holiday Inn, where President Hurst was staying, was also being run by the military.

"Quite a comedown from Villa Rose, huh?" George asked as they settled into the comfortable suite. "We can't take a chance on tarnishing your image of 'the suffering servant'!" People need to comprehend that you are one of them."

"No. Really. This is fine. I'm not above a good night's sleep, you know." He grinned as he stretched out on the bed.

It wasn't because the bed wasn't comfortable that Maxwell didn't sleep well. Each time he closed his eyes, horrible war torn visions marched into view. He got up and read over the speech he had prepared for the citizens in the Crisis Control Camps he was scheduled to visit. The speech he was to give at the Atlanta Speedway in the morning would be broadcast live around the world.

That morning Maxwell's limousine, flanked by security vehicles, formed a motorcade that moved through the quiet countryside without hindrance. Maxwell looked at a vacant landscape where the only signs of life were gigantic tractors stirring up dust as they worked the fields. "Traffic isn't as bad as it used to be," he quipped as they sped along the deserted super highway.

"Frankly, I can't wait to get myself into another traffic jam," George confided. "These last three months have been an experience that I sure in hell don't want to repeat. Ever!"

"You and a few billion others!"

When they stopped at the gate to the Camp, Control Officers greeted them with a smart salute waving them on. They entered the huge tent city that housed 100,000 people one of many that confined the citizens in this sector. If they felt imprisoned Maxwell's arrival symbolized their freedom and they welcomed him with stunning fervor.

Chants of goodwill were endless and each surging cheer swelled within him filling him with a sense of infallible power. Emotion spilled from him in the form of tears. Finally Maxwell was able to quiet them enough to begin his address.

"You have overwhelmed me!" he exclaimed. They broke into spontaneous cheers. "Your patient endurance throughout this crisis overwhelms me," he said again. "Yesterday we flew over the demolished city of Washington, D.C., and those of you who have served on recovery missions to Atlanta know the kind of devastation I'm talking about. Something like this will *never* happen again!" he promised. "***Ever!***" He had to pause again for their hearty approval.

"We are about to go out to rebuild our cities—the ones stricken by the bombs in America and Russia. We are about to rebuild those cities that were shaken down all around the world by the natural disasters that have racked this planet. The storm is over, the sun has *not* ceased to shine, and we will *not* cease to exist as a people.

We will join with all people everywhere as part of a glorious new future. As we have stated before it is our goal that every man, woman, and child have the basic rights of humanity. In order to achieve that we must all begin walking shoulder to shoulder across this broad earth. Small steps at first, baby steps, but as we link arms and march on we will become a mighty force that will cover the earth. United we can recover. United we can grow and expand until the blessings that you have enjoyed here in America become the norm throughout the world.

Within a week my family: the First Lady, our children, and I will be the first in the world to receive a life changing registration number. This momentous occasion will be broadcast live thoughout the entire world."

He paused and a hush fell over the crowd as though in a trance. "The following day," he continued, "each of you will be asked to follow our example. Your compliance will be an act of faith. Your number, as unique to you as your iris or fingerprint will become a symbol of your freedom. Freedom to enjoy all the benefits and privileges of our new system."

His countenance changed suddenly as if to communicate how dead serious he was. He leaned forward, speaking out to the unseen populations of the earth, "Don't be fooled by anyone or anything trying to hinder our plans. No one on earth or in heaven will hinder our progress! Mankind stands on the threshold of a new age—an age of peace, purpose, and prosperity. Thank you and God bless you."

Maxwell was grateful for the two cars of security agents that had been assigned to him as the crowd erupted when he closed his speech and began surging forward to touch him. It took eight men to hold them back. Maxwell managed to reach out to as many of them as possible before he was literally put in the car by the agents and driven from the camp in haste.

George was beaming. "Looks like the rest of us are going to have to take a back seat from here on out, old boy," he said slapping Maxwell on the knee. "I'm damn sure proud of you!"

Maxwell relaxed back into the plush seat. He smiled back at his friend. "I'm damn proud of myself," he thought smugly.

Neither the hovercraft tour of the demolished city of Atlanta, nor even the unimaginable magnitude of the flooding in Florida that had literally wiped that state off the map had the capacity to dim the victorious glow that burned in Maxwell's chest. The compassion that he should have felt for the displaced and lost people of those devastated places was lost to the feeling that he, *Maxwell Hurst*, was the answer to the world's woes. **He** could fix it.

CHAPTER 26

As Maxwell looked down at the landing pad at Camp David, ancient emotions stirred in his heart. This place held a forbidden secret in his personal memory bank. The one and only time he had been unfaithful to his wife was here. The girl was a vivacious and beautiful actress. As hard as he had tried, Maxwell could not resist her advances. It would have been like kicking aside an adoring kitten. He had been shocked when he had been informed of her suicide a few months after his 'assassination'.

This briefing would further inform the President concerning the implementation of the new system as it was about to be inaugurated by him and his family. After Thursday they would truly become the First Family of the United States of the World.

"How was the tour?" Paul asked, settling into one of several comfortable chairs. Maxwell thought of the vast diversity of feeling he had experienced in the last forty-eight hours. He had been brought from the depths of despair as he viewed the carnage of war to the pinnacle of personal ecstasy as he received acclaim from thousands of grateful survivors. How could he possibly put into words the answer to such a routine question as, "How was your tour?"

"It was okay." He knew that Paul, like most people, would be satisfied with that answer and move on with the conversation.

"Sure it was *okay*," Jeff chided. "From what I heard, you had them eating out of the palm of your hand." He clenched his fist as if to symbolize some secret power.

The two men exchanged knowing looks, and Maxwell realized that Jeff was probably the only other person in the room who understood what had happened to him at the Crisis Control Camp. Jeff could identify because every time he got up to preach a supernatural flow of power reached out to people. The bond between the President and the Bishop was solidified even more.

"We will rebuild on several fronts," George began, directing their attention to the wall monitor. "The first and foremost project is the rebuilding of the Temple in Jerusalem." A picture of the destroyed Mosque filled the screen. "Jerusalem must quickly become the hub on which the wheel revolves with the Temple at the very center. The Temple will symbolize our solidarity as a people."

"That's appropriate," Jeff added. "Jerusalem has been a Holy City to more than two-thirds of the world's population. The bone of contention at last becomes the pulse of the public. A rallying ground for all Nations."

"Exactly," George agreed. "It will also be a source of pride which can be shared throughout the world as Temples are erected in every region. But as crucial as the Temple is, our first priority is the teaching and indoctrination of the WORD. That, gentlemen, must never be forgotten. World Order through Religious Discipline is designed to keep a constant check on the citizens of the world. It is our complete system of Justice; it is our gospel, our Magna Carta, and our credo. Without it, we lose control; it is as simple as that."

Maxwell nodded in agreement. He had spent years studying the WORD and it was the most logical, ingenious, system of population management he had ever seen. The basic tenet of 'obedience=blessing/disobedience=curse' was meant to be used as an effective reward/discipline tool. The first test of the system would come on Friday when every person on the face of the earth would be given the opportunity to obey the first commandment and become a registered citizen of the new world.

"Getting people relocated and settled into permanent housing will be a horrendous job that will require unlimited man power," George continued. "This project can only be accomplished by the people themselves helping each other."

Paul had worked for years on the economics of the new system and now his dreams were coming to fruition. "The first step in restructuring is to forgive all debts. All real property becomes part of the system and personal wealth will be brought into the Central Treasury. From there, it will be dispersed according to the needs and well being of the corporate whole. Jobs will be plentiful, especially in these first reconstructive years.

Limited free enterprise will be encouraged on a local level, but only as supply and demand affects those within any given city or sub-region. All other needs will be supplied by the Regional Exchange, a warehouse type complex that will disperse every item needed for human consumption and use—from food, drugs, dry goods, household goods, and hardware, to even some trivia. These mega centers will not only supply our citizens with needed goods, but they will also receive locally produced goods for sale to encourage trading within the sub-region or city. All surplus products will be held by the World Trade Board and dispersed according to the needs of citizens throughout the system. Trade between regions and nations will only be carried on by the World Trade Board."

"Actually the system is a very simple one easily demonstrated by this wheel within a wheel diagram." George directed their attention once more to the monitor. "The hub represents the WORD as administered from the Temple in Jerusalem. Our President and symbol of power will reside there.

The purity of the plan will be guarded by our Bishop as authority filters down to the people through the ministry units which include: Ministry of Justice, Ministry of Agriculture, Ministry of Health, Ministry of Housing, Ministry of Trade, Ministry of Banking, Ministry of Transportation, Ministry of Communication, Ministry of Earth Keeping, Ministry of Space Exploration, and the Ministry of Peacekeeping. The governing body is made up of the Minister in Chief of each unit, the President, and the Bishop. These thirteen compromise the Council of Ministers that oversee the administration of government between the Nation States.

Each Nation is further divided into sectors, regions, and sub-regions or cities served by a Council of Administrators. Each region will share one Health Center, one Exchange, and one Temple. A region's size and shape are, of course, determined by the population and can easily be altered by relocation of citizens in order to maintain a balanced society."

All these familiar and intricate plans that had been formulated over the years were about to be tested. This was the final huddle before the last play of the big game. The ball was in their court and there was no way they could lose.

George looked at his watch. "That's about it. Are there any questions?"

"Just one," Maxwell said. "Do we have a projection date for the completion of the Temple construction? How long will we be operating from Brussels, in other words? Marion is going to hate to relinquish her rights as the Lady of Gasbeek! She loves that place."

"I'd say three to three and a half years at the most."

Paul, who was standing beside Maxwell put his hand on the President's shoulder and said in a low confiding tone, "Enough time to plan a wedding."

"What wedding?" Maxwell demanded.

"Leslie's and mine. We want you to be the first to know."

"Damn your hide, Paul. This is going to kill Marion."

"Don't worry. She'll be over the shock before you see her in Maine tomorrow. I guess I should say when *we* see her in Maine tomorrow."

"Damn you, Paul," Maxwell said again, grinning and shaking Paul's hand. "What the hell! Leslie could do worse!" he admitted and they both laughed.

CHAPTER 27

The next day Maxwell and Paul left Camp David together. They were both anxious to get to Maine. They each had a woman waiting for them. Maxwell deliberately avoided talking to Paul about his daughter. Instead, they discussed the economy, reconstruction, and politics in general. The flight to Bangor was uneventful and soon after landing they boarded a waiting hovercraft for the short trip to Bar Harbor. Paul had never been to Maine but looking down at Mount Desert Island from the air was reminiscent of his own European homeland. The lush green mountaintops and craggy bluffs suddenly gave way to the royal blue of the seashore. The hovercraft slowed, hovering momentarily, before descending gently to the landing pad beneath them. The two-story white frame house a short distance away seemed to be perched precariously close to the cliff behind it.

Marion, Leslie, and Max walked out across the immaculately trimmed lawn to greet them. Suddenly Leslie was rushing ahead of the others and Paul lifted her into his waiting arms. He kissed her full on the lips, oblivious to what her parents might think.

It was a poignant reunion for the Maxwell and Marion as well. Coming home after so many years was an emotional apex not easily surmounted.

"Welcome to Acadia," Max said shaking Paul's hand. "You are going to love it here. Are you a horseman?" he asked motioning toward the stables.

"Yes, I love to ride," he answered. "Quite an estate you have here," he added noticing several other buildings nestled neatly around the main house.

"I am dying to show you the Island," Leslie said, pulling him closer to her side. "It is the most beautiful place on the face of the earth!"

As they approached the house, Paul saw a small group of people around the garden pool. "What is this? A welcoming committee?" he asked cheerfully.

"Aunts, uncles, and cousins," Marion explained. "This has been a wonderful reunion for us. It's as though that nasty war business had never happened."

"Until you take a tour as I did," Maxwell said.

"Or wander down to Bar Harbor," Max added. "Jeez, what an eerie feeling. No-body around. All the unique little shops that were always crawling with tourists, deserted! The locals are all still inland at Crisis Camps."

"That will change soon," Maxwell promised. "Until then, I intend to enjoy the next few days to the hilt!"

Paul was graciously accepted by the extended family and the eating and drinking eventually lead to a mellow evening under the stars with dancing in the moonlight. Partners were exchanged often and it was just a matter of time before Marion found herself in Paul's arms. Marion's head felt light as Paul turned her smoothly in waltzing swirls. He smiled down at her with the same charming smile that had melted her heart in the past.

"Well, how do you feel?"

"What do you mean? How do I feel?"

"How do you feel about me marrying Leslie?"

She hoped he couldn't read the pain in her eyes as she answered. "I'm getting used to the idea, but I'm not sure it makes me happy."

"I'm giving her a ring tomorrow." He paused, "I want you to be happy for us, Marion. Can you do that?"

She saw the pain in his eyes or perhaps it was a reflection of her own agony. "She's so young."

Marion wanted to say more but he cut her off. "Marion, let go," he pleaded. "It's been over for years, just let go." Paul was gripping her tightly now, speaking close to her ear. "You belong to Maxwell. You are part of his future. I want you to be as happy as I intend to be with Leslie. I love her, you know. Not just because she is a part of you, but truly, I love her for herself. I promise, I'll make her happy."

Marion fought hard to hold back the tears that threatened to spill down her cheeks. "I know you will, Paul," she said accepting her defeat. "I know you will. I love you Paul. I love you *both*."

Accepting her resignation, he pulled her close for one last reassuring hug. The waltz was finished and they were both smiling when Paul delivered Marion into Maxwell's arms and claimed his own prize triumphantly.

Acadia at sun up, Paul discovered, was a close rival to Acadia in moonlight. Paul and Leslie enjoyed a leisurely breakfast on the front porch overlooking the sea. The surf lapping the rocks below, gulls circling high above, and the warm rays of an early summer sun began the first of three unforgettable days for them. This day would be the most special because Paul planned to find the perfect spot to propose properly and present Leslie with the diamond ring he carried in his vest pocket.

A riding tour, a picnic lunch, and a romantic location were the perfect ingredients for the special event. Leslie, who knew her childhood home well was an excellent tour guide as well as an exceptional horsewoman. The system of carriage roads wound through damp green forests, through fertile valleys, and under quaint stone bridges. They rode to the top of Cadillac Mountain, the highest point on the entire Atlantic coast. From it's barren windy top, they could see the entire Island in all of its rugged diversity.

"Look," Leslie said, pointing to a golden ribbon of sand far below. "That's Sand Beach, my favorite spot on the entire Island."

"Well, what are we waiting for?" Paul asked as he turned his mount toward the winding mountain road. The trek down was much faster than the climb up and they reached the beach around mid-day. Approaching an elegant abandoned, seaside inn Paul dismounted and lifted Leslie from her horse. Together they explored the premises.

"Ah ha!" Paul exclaimed as he lifted an open window and climbed easily through. Once inside he opened the glass doors that faced the sea and Leslie joined him.

"Let's find someplace to eat. I'm famished." She looked around at the dining room and declared, "This room is too big."

"Come on then, let's find something more intimate."

She laughed as he pulled her along from room to room. All the ground floor guest rooms faced the sea and each had individual gardens. Paul dusted off a small round patio table and two chairs and began to lie out the lunch from the basket.

"This is perfect. Let me see if the champagne is still chilled. Ah, yes, my lady. Please rest yourself here." He gestured grandly for Leslie to be seated as he began to work carefully on the cork. He poured the sparkling wine into the stemmed glasses that he had brought and placed them on the table. Ignoring the fact that he may look very silly to Leslie, he proceeded to get down on one knee before her. He drew a small velvet box out of his vest pocket. He opened it and took out the ring, and then he took her hand gently in his and looked into her eyes. "Leslie," he asked, while placing the ring on her finger, "will you honor me by becoming my wife?"

She didn't laugh. She didn't even smile, but said in all seriousness, "Yes, Paul, I will be honored to become your wife."

He stood and pulled her to her feet. He handed her the glass of champagne. "To our future."

"To our future," she repeated. He kissed her tenderly, longingly, but with self-control. He could and would wait, although not without regret.

After a long, lazy afternoon lying on the warm sandy beach planning and dreaming, they promised each other that they would consummate their wedding vows at this lovely inn.

After three memorable days at Acadia, the family prepared to fly to Bangor for the registration ceremony. The event would be broadcast live sending the historic moment instantly around the world.

"You were right, darling," Paul said to Leslie as they boarded the hovercraft. "This is the most beautiful place in the world."

"We'll come back soon," she promised him.

"All set then, Mr. President?" the pilot asked Maxwell.

"All set. Take it away."

They gazed down in silence as Acadia receded until even the Island itself was just a glowing memory.

Chapter 28

As the hovercraft landed at the Crisis Control Camp on the outskirts of Bangor, a vast cheering crowd gathered to greet them.

"They seem very happy to see us," Leslie commented.

"They are," Maxwell stated. "It means they will soon be free to return to their homes."

"*If* they comply," Max added. "Do you think they will, Dad?"

"I sure hope so, Max"

"What happens if they don't?"

"They will." Maxwell didn't want to think about the possibility that some may have to be incarcerated. Not today. "Anyone would have to be crazy *not* to cooperate with a system as equitable and humane as our new world will be," he thought.

Ten ominous looking mobile units had been quietly pulled into the camp during the night. The units had one entrance, one exit, and no windows. The cheering crowd watched as the first family approached the ramp and prepared to enter. Maxwell turned toward them and an eerie hush fell as he lifted his arm and waved. The door slid silently open and the four of them disappeared inside. Cameras captured every second of the registration process and sent the news reeling around the globe.

A Control Officer sat at a desk before a huge, shiny computer. A voice, not unlike CC's, directed them to a short, narrow corridor that led directly through the center of the machine. Maxwell hesitated momentarily, "What had the so called messenger said about a mark?" He shrugged as he stepped into the narrow chamber, "That's a lot of crap!" he thought.

The whizzing and clicking machine quietly adjusted itself until Maxwell's head was imprisoned in some sort of mechanized headgear. He heard another unfamiliar sound and within seconds he was released and free to walk out on the other side.

"Please step into the red circle, Mr. President," another Control Officer seated at a second computer said. As he stepped into the circle a number appeared on the screen and Maxwell realized he had just been scanned. His number began with a code 6 representing the world, his nation state, and his region, followed by his own personal numerical signature, 666. The red circle turned green and a mechanical voice said, "You may exit now." As he exited the unit he was handed a book by still a third Control Officer who recorded the transaction on a third computer. The whole procedure had taken less than two minutes.

Maxwell waited as one by one his family emerged from the back of the unit just as he had.

"Can you see anything on my forehead, Mom?" Leslie asked.

"No, not a thing. It is there though, I saw it on the monitor."

"That was tough," Max, laughed as Paul emerged last.

The camera was still running as the first family climbed the stairs to the temporary stage where Maxwell was scheduled to deliver a greeting to the anxiously waiting citizens of the world. The thousands gathered before the stage clapped wildly. Maxwell looked down on the adoring crowd and motioned for silence. "We stand before you as the very first citizens of the United States of the World." He put his arm around Marion and drew her close. "We, myself, my wife, and our children, are proud to be the first of many."

The crowd went wild again. Maxwell felt his heart swell within his chest. He gripped Marion tighter. They looked at each other and tears of joy spilled shamelessly down Marion's face as she sensed the magnitude of the moment.

Maxwell lifted his hands for silence.

"At sunrise tomorrow every one of you can take the simple step that we did here today. Every Crisis Control Camp in the world will have these same mobile units like the one you saw us enter. Each one is equipped with the technology to painlessly register each one of you. As you walk out the back exit you will be given a copy of the WORD." He held up his own personal copy. "This book is the most valuable possession you will leave with tomorrow. Your very first obligation in the free world is that you open this book to the first page and begin to read it. You must not only read it, but you must also act on it. If the book says sit down, *sit down*. If the book says stand up, *stand up*. This is as crucial as life and death itself. The Ministry Unit of the WORD will ensure that you each understand what is expected of you. Weekly seminars will be required." He smiled and said reassuringly," Don't worry, this will not be drudgery. Think of the benefits of such a society: law and order, jobs for everyone, plenty to eat, a roof over your head, medical and dental benefits, education, and best of all, *no more war!"*

When he said "no more war" the crowd erupted again into shouts and cheers. He had to calm them again to finish his speech.

"My dear friends, don't ever forget. I am here for you. I gave up the prime of my life *for* you and I dedicate the rest of my life *to* you." His last words were fraught with emotion and he couldn't continue, but it didn't really matter, the mass of cheering humanity had lost control.

The Hurst family waved good-bye to the thundering sea of adoring fans and Maxwell would have been truly overwhelmed if he could have somehow received the adoration that was being generated from Camps around the world: from one end of the globe to the other.

Multitudes were more than willing to follow in his exemplary footsteps in spite of dire warnings from small groups of dissenters in each camp. When dawn marched across the earth the next morning the majority of humanity lined up eagerly and was quickly and painlessly initiated into the *United States of the World*.

CHAPTER 29

Maxwell woke up first. Marion slept peacefully beside him in spite of the sunlight that poured into the room. He sat on the edge of the bed shaking his head to clear out the grog. "These international flights are taking their toll," he thought. He pushed a button and the drapes moved silently across the huge circular window closing out the misty green of the rolling countryside that surrounded Gasbeek.

He closed the dressing room door quietly and when he was ready to leave, he kissed his wife lightly. She stirred and murmured, "Is it morning already?"

"Yes, but you sleep awhile. I'm going over to the command center. When I get back, we'll have breakfast."

"Ummm," she murmured snuggling deeper into the soft satin sheets.

Paul was already at the Center monitoring the registration process. "Good morning, Maxwell," he said cheerfully. "Have a good night?"

"Very good, thanks. Just not enough of it. How are things going?" he asked as he looked at the screens that filled the room.

"For the most part, exceptionally well. We do have dissidents in every camp but they are mostly radical Christians. They have been having a field day since the UFO affair. It seems they are preaching that the UFO incident was an angelic warning not to cooperate in the registration."

"So they don't buy the idea that Russia was behind the incident?"

"Apparently not."

"They don't know our capability, that's all," Maxwell said, leaning back in his chair to think. Okay, why don't we show them a little of our capability?" he asked, leaning in toward Paul. "Let's bring out an XTZ for a little show of our own. Get me a Code Six; let's see what they think."

Both men, George in Mount Weather and Rolph at Thera listened as Maxwell explained the proposal.

"Sounds like a good idea to me," George offered.

"I especially like the idea of a visual *and* audio communication," Rolph said. It will more likely convince those that are looking for a sign from their space god."

"I'll contact Nevada today," George promised.

"Why don't you suggest the XTZ?" Maxwell suggested.

"The XTZ would be perfect. I'm on it. In the meantime get Jeff to record a message. Tell him we are going on with this tonight."

"Sounds good." The Code Six was concluded and Maxwell turned to Paul. "Get Jeff over here and fill him in. I'm going back to have breakfast with Marion."

"Right away, sir," Paul said with an informal salute.

Marion was up and dressed when he returned. He filled her in on the morning's proceedings while they ate.

"What will happen to the people who refuse to register?"

"They will be sent to Confinement Centers."

"You mean prisons?"

"No, not exactly. Since most of the dissidents are Christians that refused to become a part of the ecumenical movement, they will be housed in the Free Churches that they built after Unity." He poured the rich, steaming Belgium coffee into his cup. "They will be allowed to return to their homes to pack up their belongings. We are giving them forty-eight hours before they must report to their assigned Center."

"You see, you do mean Prison!" Marion said, disturbed.

"Look, darling, all they need to do is agree to registration. At any time, day or night, they can walk out free men and women. Now, let me ask you— w*ho* is putting them in prison?"

As darkness fell across the earth the mission of XTZ, code named Ecstasy, became a spectacular display over near empty camps everywhere. Impressive visuals accompanied Jeff's message, "My children, hear my voice and obey. The Kingdom of Peace has come to earth. Have no fear for it is the will of God that you suffer not. It is the will of God for your prosperity. Again I say, children, hear my voice and obey," The charade was as heavenly as humanly possible. The technology was stunning, high speed maneuvering complete with weird and unearthly sound effects. In spite of the blitz, most of those left in the camps stood fast, ignoring elaborate efforts to convince them to register. They boldly declared that their own Bibles had warned them of such a deception.

The following morning the camps were dismantled. Small groups of people with their meager belongings were herded together and given orders. "You will be bussed to your old neighborhood to pack up what you can and be transported to your assigned Confinement Center." All very orderly. All very voluntary.

Chapter 30

"This is very disturbing," Maxwell said studying the reports. "Seven hundred million people have chosen to reject the system! That's almost fifteen percent of the world's population!"

"Look at it from the other perspective," Paul said. "Over eighty-five percent have embraced the new order. On top of that, we can expect converts as the screw is turned and things begin to get a little tight."

"You're right. When they see us in action they will want to get on the band wagon and share the pie."

"But, Dad, it seems really cruel to incarcerate people and not provide for them. They'll starve to death."

"That's a possibility, Max, but if we try to feed them we will be going right back into the welfare state we just scrapped."

"It is not as though they will have no resources at all. They will have buildings to occupy and they have been given the opportunity to outfit their Centers with their own property—provided it is clear of any debt," Paul explained.

"And don't forget," Maxwell added with tongue in cheek, "They have a God who will supply all their needs. Or so they claim!"

"That *will* be interesting," Paul said. "In the meantime, we do have a few billion people that we need to consider and they are who I intend to concentrate on. I doubt that a handful of dissidents can cause much of a stir, although they made a fair attempt yesterday when they refused to co-operate."

"I, for one, don't plan to lose much sleep over them. All their dire warnings over the past weeks have had little impact on the masses," Maxwell said, picking up the report. It was clear he meant to get down to business.

"Our first concern is reconstruction and relocation. The Ministry of Housing is handling that. Hopefully our citizens in overpopulated areas will cooperate with relocation plans. If not, they will simply be moved by decree. On another front we have begun construction on the Temple in Jerusalem. If we are going to nail down an ecclesiastical union between the three ecumenical streams we will need to do it quickly. Jeff is already on the job in Jerusalem and we are getting it together here in Brussels."

Maxwell placed a hand on his son's shoulder. "Max, how would you like to go to Thera and work with Rolph managing registration records for all the Confinement Centers?"

"Would I? Super!"

"It will be a big job. Do you think you can handle it?"

"I *know* I can handle it, Dad, thanks!"

"You'll work in Greece for the most part, but right now Paul needs you here in Brussels."

"Whatever you say. I'm ready to go." Max was overjoyed at the prospect of going back to Villa Rose.

"CC's data will constantly need updating as citizens are upgraded and relocated. We'll also have to maintain data about each dissident and where we can find them: the Sector, Region, and Confinement Center. Each individual will be assigned a permanent ID number so when he or she decides to comply with registration, all you'll have to do is add a Code Six. With this system, we can find anyone in any Center anywhere on the face of the earth. Ingenious, huh?"

"That's pretty awesome all right," Max had to agree, "but not surprising given the realm of computer science."

"It's lunch time," Paul noted, looking at his watch. "Let's not keep the ladies waiting."

"By all means," Maxwell agreed, as the three of them left the Command Center for the short walk across the garden.

Marion and Leslie were waiting on the veranda. It was a beautiful summer day. A gentle breeze ruffled the leaves on the vines that wove themselves into the latticework above them screening out the heat of a noonday sun.

Leslie arose to greet Paul, who lovingly placed an arm around her waist and whispered in her ear, "Miss me?"

"Of course," she replied, smiling brightly.

Maxwell leaned down and kissed his wife on the cheek. "Have a good morning?" he asked as he joined them at the table.

"Very restful, thank you, dear."

"Mom, guess what? Dad is giving me a job! I am going to work with Rolph managing the data for the Confinement Centers. I'll live at Villa Rose."

"Is this true, Maxwell?"

"Yes it's true." Maxwell was proud of his son's brilliant ability with the machines that were destined to mold the future of the planet.

"Congratulations, darling," Marion said leaning to kiss her son who had seated himself beside her. "This calls for a celebration."

" Phillip," she said to a waiter who was placing platters laden with food on the table. "Will you be kind enough to bring us a bottle of champagne?"

"Right away, madame," he said scurrying off to do her bidding.

"Mmm, that was delicious," Max, said, pushing back his plate and picking up his half empty glass of champagne. "Okay, so, Dad, when can I leave for Thera?"

"Well not until next week, at least. The Confinement Centers are being outfitted with their machines, but it will take most of this week to get everything set up. In the meantime, Paul has plenty of work for you downtown."

Max had seen the mega computer downtown only once and from that exposure he fully understood why they called it the "Beast".

"I'll be leaving in the morning to fly to Jerusalem to meet with Jeff and George, but I should be back before you have to leave."

"Don't anybody leave until Paul and I have our say!" Leslie interrupted. "Dad, Mom, Paul and I would like to talk about a date for our wedding. We are thinking about June."

"June! Next June?" Maxwell seemed surprised.

"Why does June surprise you?" Paul asked. "I thought most American weddings were solemnized in June."

"I had hoped that you two would be the first to marry in the new Temple in Jerusalem."

"But Daddy," protested Leslie, "they've barely begun construction on the Temple. When will it be finished?"

"Spring, 2025."

"That's almost three years. Well, that settles it. We are *not* going to be married in Jerusalem!"

Paul raised his eyebrows and shrugged his shoulders in complete subjection to Leslie's wishes. Wherever the location, it would not be too soon for him. He was getting impatient to have her as his own.

Marion, who had been listening silently, suddenly smiled brightly. "I have a suggestion. Why not have the wedding in Rome?"

"*Rome?*"

"Yes, Rome," her mother repeated, "at the Basilica!"

"Saint Peter's?" Maxwell asked incredulously. A smile spread across his face. "Marion, that's a brilliant idea. They *should* be married in Rome. At the Basilica!"

Leslie and Paul agreed heartily. Max didn't care. The champagne was passed around again and they toasted the upcoming June wedding in Rome.

CHAPTER 31

The next morning, Maxwell and George, flew to Jerusalem to meet with Jeff. The Ecumenical Movement was in the final stages of evolution. As impossible as it had seemed twenty five years ago the wide diverse rivers of theology had been refined into three basic streams: the Christians, the Muslims, and the Jews, and now Jeff was presiding over the meetings that were crucial to the completion of the system.

Jeff was more than ready to relax after a long day of deliberations. Maxwell and George had spent the day on the Temple Mount watching the construction there. It had been quite a day for all three of them.

"Well, we agree on the most important and fundamental doctrine," Jeff said as they unwound with an after dinner brandy. "One sovereign God." He put his glass down. "We also each acknowledge the fact that we have the same ancestral lineage, Father Abraham."

"Yes, and the Temple itself will be a common icon to bind us together," Maxwell offered.

"This is true," Jeff agreed. "By the way, how is construction coming along?"

"Very well," George replied. "Things are right on schedule. The foundation work is nearly finished. Oh, how I envy you, Jeff, watching the progress from day to day."

"You will find plenty of occasions to visit Jerusalem, George."

"I'm not as spry as I used to be. Old age I guess."

Maxwell and Jeff looked at their friend. It was true. It seemed that George had become ancient just since their last meeting, a common occurrence with aging.

"No, now that I've retired, I have this overwhelming desire to just sit. So sit, I do."

"You better get rested up so you can attend Leslie and Paul's wedding next spring. They plan to be married in June."

"Wonderful news!" George exclaimed. "In Brussels?"

"No, in Rome."

"In Rome?" Jeff inquired.

"Yes, at Saint Peter's. We thought it would be a nice touch. Marion and I were Roman Catholics you know."

"Yes, I know and you couldn't pick a more grand or historical location."

"I agree," George said, "and if I am alive, I'll be there with bells on," he promised.

That night, Maxwell had a hard time sleeping. If he had been at Gasbeek, he would have pulled his sweet Marion into his arms for comfort, but here he was alone and lonely. The night was sweltering. He got up and went out on the balcony to think. He thought of George and how old he had seemed that night. "Hell. He *is* old! We all are!" That thought depressed him even more. From where he stood, he could look to the east and see the Temple Mount. He saw the sun begin to rise behind it. "Damn," he thought. "I haven't slept at all." He looked at his watch. Two a.m.. He went inside and checked the clock on the nightstand. "Two a.m.," he read. Maxwell returned to the balcony and watched as the light behind the horizon got larger and even more brilliant. Suddenly the luminous globe burst forth and bobbed gently above the Temple mount.

Maxwell knew instantly that this was *not* the sun, and the hairs on the back of his neck bristled as he watched in amazement. The light intensified and elongated into a familiar, softly feminine shape. Maxwell fell to his knees in adoration. He felt himself bathed in warmth that enveloped his very being and he knew without raising his head that the apparition had approached him.

He heard her melodious voice, rich and confiding, "My dear son, I have been sent to bring to fulfillment the plans of the Divine Master. You will restore devotion to my Sacred Heart. You will heed my voice. The Three *shall* become One. The One shall become *Thee*."

At that same moment, Maxwell felt a tremendous surge of power throughout his body as though some mysterious force had touched him. He dared to lift his head and look at her beauty. She seemed to loom above him in all her glory. She was robed in scarlet and on her head was a crown encrusted with precious jewels. A voice, not hers, thundered in his head. "Behold The Queen of Heaven. Hear Her." As quickly as she came she was gone and Maxwell stood shaking in the sudden darkness. The chilly night air enveloped him and he retreated to the warmth of his bed. Miraculously he went to sleep immediately and slept like a baby.

The Clerics were not so fortunate. They each awoke and witnessed the apparition in their separate quarters. Sleep did not come for any of them that night.

George did not see the vision. His breath left him as he slept, and he lay dead in his bed. He would, after all, miss the wedding in Rome.

The morning meeting was convened amidst an aura of underlying excitement. Bit by bit, each became aware of the corporate experience of the night vision.

"I was mysteriously awakened at two a.m." the Rabbi shared. "It was as though the sun was beginning to rise in the east."

"And then this brilliant light over the Temple Mount," finished the Iman.

"The Three shall become One," Jeff added. "Nothing can stop us now," he thought.

It didn't matter when Maxwell interrupted the proceedings. The details of the Ecumenical Union would now be a matter of formality. Three streams had suddenly become one mighty river that would flow out to the world from Jerusalem. Maxwell bent close to Jeff's ear and informed him of George's passing.

"My friends," Jeff announced, "I have just learned the sad news that our dear colleague, George Middleton, has passed away in his sleep." He looked very distraught. "We will suspend our meeting until further notice. I expect you gentlemen to stay in Jerusalem indefinitely to cement our alliance." He bowed slightly, then hurried out with Maxwell.

Arrangements were made for the funeral held in Brussels. It was attended by dignitaries from around the world and afterward George's ashes were then flown back to his hometown near Washington D.C. for internment.

The rest of them went to Gasbeek: the Hurst family, Paul, Jeff, Mikeal, and Rolph. They mourned the passing of a man that had not only been instrumental in molding history, but a dear and close friend. They comforted each other.

Chapter 32

The experience shared by the spiritual leaders gathered in Jerusalem sealed their unity. The formula for creating an ecclesiastical profile for the new system became crystal clear. One God, yet three: God the Father embodied in the Jewish constituent, God the Son embodied in the Christian constituent, and God the Holy Spirit embodied in the Islamic constituent. They declared three days holy: Friday, Saturday, and Sunday. They recognized one holy place, the newly resurrected Temple in Jerusalem. They shared one holy city, Jerusalem. They pointed back to one mortal ancestor, Abraham. They venerated one Holy Mother, the Queen of Heaven. They acknowledged one Holy Book, the WORD. And lastly, they unanimously agreed to accept Archbishop Jefferson Brandon Richards to speak for them.

Jeff's spirit was infectious. "Maxwell, if things get much better, you may need to nail me to the floor. Every problem we set out to tackle just melts like a wrinkle under a hot iron. Honestly, it's incredible!"

Maxwell laughed at Jeff's exuberance. "I know exactly what you mean. But don't worry, you won't float off into space. You are tethered to success just like the rest of us. I'm proud of you, Jeff. I'm proud of us. We are a team, a damn good team!"

They both laughed as they finished their brandy. Jeff set down the glass and said, "Let's get over to the construction site. That's what you came for. A busy man like yourself can't afford to stay too long in one place."

Jeff's job was here in Jerusalem cementing the world in the spiritual realm while it was Maxwell's task to cement them politically by visiting nation after nation on goodwill missions.

"Construction is right on schedule," Jeff told Maxwell. The immense structure, now just a skeleton of its future glory, was beginning to take shape as thousands of construction workers from every nation shared the work. Many more were involved as architects, artisans, interior decorators, weavers, agricultural specialists, machinists, scholars, musicians, merchants, and indeed every kind of professional known to modern man. The Temple was evolving into a hub of collective pride throughout the entire world system.

"Will all this be ready for World Day?"

"Most certainly, Mr. President."

"What about the Sector Temples? How is the progress on that level?"

"That's all right on schedule. Don't worry, Maxwell, the job will be done. Honestly, it is real spooky the way everything is falling into place. I speak, they jump! I mean it is super spooky!"

"That's the way it should be. It is our destiny, you know. Yours and mine, I mean. We have been chosen for this very purpose."

The two men looked at each other. Jeff saw the power in the eyes of his friend. They stared at each other for a long moment and Jeff was so consumed that he had to look away, unaware that Maxwell saw a similar power in the eyes of the Archbishop.

"What the hell?" Jeff exclaimed, breaking the spell.

Maxwell swung around and looked to where Jeff was pointing. He saw a huge saucer shaped craft hovering silently over the Temple site. "Holy shit! They're back!"

Jeff pulled one of the workers aside. "Do you see something up there?" he asked.

The man removed his hard hat and looked up, "Son of a bitch!" he muttered shading his eyes from the glare of the thing.

One by one all the workers stopped their labor and were gazing up at the craft above them.

"I'm going to contact the Minister of Defense," Maxwell said turning to leave.

"It's gone," Jeff whispered.

Maxwell turned back around and looked up. Sure enough it was nowhere in sight. "Did you see it leave?"

"No, it moved so fast it seemed to just disappear," Jeff said, "I don't believe we have that capability."

When Maxwell contacted the Minister of Defense, he was informed that there had been more than one sighting like the one Maxwell described. Mostly above Confinement Centers.

"If these sightings have occurred why haven't I been made aware of it?" Maxwell demanded.

The embarrassing oversight would not go unpunished in spite of promises to keep the President informed in the future.

"Don't let this happen again," Maxwell warned. "Set up a briefing. I want to see what you have."

"Yes, sir. When will you be back in Brussels?"

"In the morning. Set up a meeting after lunch," Maxwell said tersely, ending the conversation.

Chapter 33

Maxwell went directly to the Berlymont upon his arrival in Brussels to meet with the Minister of Defense. The General handed the reports to Maxwell. "We have three official sightings, sir: one in Africa, one in Germany, and one in the United States."

"Thank you, General Sikes. Relax. I'm not going to chew you up and spit you out. But from now on out I must be kept informed. Do you understand?"

"Yes, sir."

"Uumm, each one reports an unidentified hovering craft. That's all? Nothing else?"

"That's it, sir."

"Well, keep me informed, General. I want you to give this top priority. If this keeps up, I'll call a joint meeting. In the meantime just keep me informed." Maxwell extended his hand, which the general shook before giving the President a smart salute.

"Darling! Welcome home. I didn't expect you until tomorrow." Marion got up from their bed where she and Leslie had spread out samples of lace.

Leslie smiled as she watched her parents embrace. "Hi, Dad. Glad you're back."

"It's good to be back," he confessed, kissing his daughter on the cheek. "How are the wedding plans coming along? Where's Paul, by the way, I didn't see him downtown."

"No, he's here in the Computer Complex. Something to do with Max and Rolph." Leslie squenched up her nose and gestured grandly. "Something mysterious."

"Probably planning a bachelor party," Marion teased.

"Probably," Maxwell agreed. "And since you two are so busy, I'll just hop on over to the complex and see what's up."

"All right, dear. We'll see you at dinner. Give my love to Max."

The March wind was brisk and Maxwell quickened his step as he crossed the expanse of the courtyard.

"Maxwell!" Paul stated, enthusiastically, as they shook hands, "we didn't expect you back today."

"Something came up. I had to cut it short." He glanced at the monitor where the image of his son was on tap. "Hello, son," he said.

"Oh, hi Dad. I didn't know you were home."

"I came back early. What's up?"

"Some really strange things are going on. Dad, do you remember reading about a group of young people predicting the war and the earthquakes? You know, *before* it all happened?"

"Yes, in fact George had the group investigated. He had the feeling that they knew more about our plans than was humanly possible. Why?"

"Well some of those same guys live in one of the Centers that I monitor in the United States. I've gotten to know two of them pretty well. They just happen to be brothers. We chat all the time."

"So?"

"They've got some screwy ideas. They told me that they are being taken care of," Max paused as though reluctant to go on, "by *angels*!"

"*Angels*!" Maxwell laughed. "Did you say angels?"

"Yes, and that's not all. They have a garden that they claim never ceases to produce. He also says that a spring suddenly appeared in the ground and fresh water bubbles out continuously."

"Oh, this is rich! You certainly don't believe any of that garbage do you?"

"I don't know, Dad," Max confessed, "I guess I would have to see it for myself."

"That might not be such a bad idea, Max. Why don't you do just that!"

"You mean go to America?"

"Yes, you could visit several Sectors while you are there. I'll send you on an official mission. You can inspect the progress on the Temple projects."

Max turned to Rolph. "Can you manage without me?"

"Sure," Rolph smiled, "as long as it doesn't take *too* long."

"All right then, it's settled," said Maxwell. I'll work up an itinerary and send it to you this week. Can you get away the first of next week?"

"Yes! Fine." Max was more than excited about the prospect of traveling abroad.

"Oh, by the way, Max, your mother sends her love. Which reminds me, I promised her that Paul and I would meet them for dinner."

"Okay, Dad. We'll talk later. Bye."

The screen went blank. For close families like the Hursts, turning off a monitor was as hard as hanging up a phone had been in the past.

Paul led the way to the dining room where Leslie and Marion waited. He kissed his fiancé and gave Marion a brief hug.

"Did you give Max my love?" she asked her husband as they all sat down.

"Sure did and he returns it ten fold. What's for dinner? I'm famished."

While they ate, Maxwell told the women about his plans to send Max to America. Then the conversation turned to the reason for his early return from Jerusalem. "What do you think, Paul? Are we being watched by aliens from outer space or what?"

"I believe there is a conspiracy underway to foil the progress we are making. All during the race for space years, Russia was clothed in secrecy. She could have easily developed the technology we are witnessing today. Just look at where our own space program has taken us, more to the point, look where *it is* taking us! Within five years we will be capable of colonizing Jupiter. It isn't a secret that Russia was leaps and bounds ahead of the rest of the world in this field."

"So you believe they are still resisting?"

"It wouldn't surprise me."

"Well, the Ministry of Defense is on it. I saw General Sikes this afternoon and we have made it a top priority."

"How could the Russians get away with something like that right under your nose?" Marion asked. "Everyone on the face of the planet is monitored like a hawk."

"There are still ways, my dear. We still have vast wilderness areas in Russia, China, and even the United States. There will always be a few who remain unhappy with *any* system of government. It is the few, however, who are dangerous."

"At one time Russia even had an outpost on the Moon. That was before we realized the danger in polluting the stratosphere," Paul added. "It isn't very likely, but it *is* a possibility that Russia has a moon base."

"Can we *please* change the subject," Leslie pleaded. "Now that we are all in the same room I want to talk about the wedding *before* Dad goes shooting off to god knows where again!"

"You watch your tongue, young lady," Maxwell said shaking his finger in his daughter's direction. "While I was *shooting* around out there, I shot by Rome. Everything is secured and ready at the Basilica."

"Oh, Dad! Thanks. Do they know that we plan to come the week prior to the ceremony?"

"They do, and they are prepared to treat you royally."

They all knew what that meant. Since Maxwell's inauguration in Brussels, which was more like a coronation, they had all been treated like royalty. Every wish and whim was granted. Planning a huge wedding was a dream come true. Marion only had to pick up the phone and people came in steady streams to serve her. Caterers, seamstresses, florists, or clergy all were at her beck and call. She and Leslie had spent long lazy months together planning the wedding that promised to be the most beautiful and lavish that anyone could imagine.

Paul looked lovingly at the two women, both so special, caught up as they were in the excitement of the event. He reached over and took Leslie's hand in his own. She smiled at the intensity in his gaze. All he could think of these days was Acadia and Sand Beach. It had been a long wait, but it would be over soon.

Chapter 34

The Presidential Jet landed smoothly at Metro Atlanta South, and Max boarded a Hovercraft for his trip to New Salem. Max was fascinated by the unfolding landscape below him. He had never been in this part of the United States, although he had read about it in history books and novels while in school. Even the movies he had seen failed to reflect the Deep South as it appeared to him today. The low rolling hills were dotted with pine forests separated by red, cultivated fields, and lazy little towns. The scene below was vastly different from the mountains of Maine or Belgium.

New Salem was actually a small city. Industry here was concentrated in three major fields: agricultural, with peanuts, pecans, strawberries, sweet potatoes, soybeans, cotton, and watermelon constituting the main crops; the Textile Industry, with a host of cotton mills and garment factories; and agricultural research, with one of the largest and most respected experiment facilities in the world located nearby. New Salem also had the distinction of being the Hub of the Region. The Central Control Office, Hospital and Medical Center, Exchange, and Temple, which was still under construction, were all located here.

Spring had come to New Salem and the city was awash in color. The live oaks, with tender, new, pinkish green leaves, lined the wide, quiet streets and gave livid contrast to the deep green pines that seemed to be everywhere. Redbud trees, along with the white lace blooms of peach, cherry, and dogwood were tucked here and there like highlights in an exquisite painting.

Azalea bushes ablaze with color ranging from light pink to deep fuchsia graced the lawns like so many dollops of strawberry ice cream.

Once on the ground, a high ranking Control Officer assigned to accompany Max as he toured the Control Centers and the Temple construction site, greeted Max.

"I'm Officer Hamby," he said, first saluting smartly then offering his hand in a more friendly gesture.

"You have a beautiful little city here. This is my first trip to the South. I'm really impressed!"

"This is the best time of the year for a visit. Spring is wonderful. It won't last long though, then the summer heat can be almost unbearable."

"Air conditioning is a life saver, I suppose."

"A life saver indeed."

The short drive to the downtown hotel was a pleasant one, but Max was happy to arrive and was more than happy to be settled in a comfortable room to relax before dinner. Later he would review the short speech he was to deliver to the dignitaries from the Region. Even though Max's major in college had been Political Science, he was never comfortable in this role. He much preferred the non-threatening atmosphere of the Computer Complex at Villa Rose. He was, in fact, fast becoming a recluse. If it weren't for his insistent curiosity about a certain Control Center here and his association with the Foster brothers, he would not be here now.

Max managed to make it through a boring evening of political rhetoric, and a peaceful nights sleep brought him, with anticipation, into a new day. Officer Hamby picked him up in the forenoon to escort him to the Center.

"I understand you manage the stats on these people?" he said. "You probably know more about them than I do. About all I know is what I hear and what I see as I patrol the area."

"Do they give your unit any trouble?"

"Not much. They *have* been known to sneak out once in a while. Word has it they have an underground network of sorts. Most of their activity is harmless though. A little barter, exchanging news, and so on."

"So you don't see them as a threat to our society?"

"Given the way they are dispersed, I'd say no; at least, not any kind of military threat. They do wage war on an ideological level though."

"What do you mean?"

"This is the type of propaganda they put out," he said, picking up a leaflet from the console beside him.

Max looked at the leaflet with a cross on the front and read the bold print beneath it. "THE SIGN", he read out loud.

"These are all quotations from their Bible," Hamby explained. "It talks about a literal appearance of their Christ."

Max believed, as did most people, that there would not be a literal appearance or "second coming" as these leaflets stated. The prophet Christ came, set up the Kingdom of God, and is presently working with all the great prophets to bring about its full inception. God is in control. The success of the ecumenical movement was proof of that. Without divine intervention, it would have been impossible to unite the ideologies of such a diverse world!

"This is wild! They numerate these *signs* that are supposed to appear in the sky to warn mankind. The heavens will shake. The moon and stars will not give their light. And this last one. The sign of the Son of Man shall appear. What sign?"

"Doesn't it say what sign?"

"No. It ends with a warning about not being deceived and quotes some verses from their Bible."

"This is the place," Hamby announced, pulling into a circular drive in front of an old brick church. A wire fence enclosed the property. "Why don't you ask them what the Sign means? They seem to have all the answers," he chuckled.

The compound consisted of three buildings connected by a covered walkway. Between the buildings was a large grassy courtyard and Max noticed a small pool of bubbling water in the very center. "That must be the spring they told me about," Max thought. "This place seems deserted."

They were about to enter a door marked 'office' when it opened and a surprised middle-aged man stood before them.

"Oh! Hello!" he said.

"We were going to knock," Max apologized. "We didn't mean to startle you."

"We are looking for Pastor Cline," Officer Hamby stated.

"I am Pastor Cline. What can I do for you?"

"This is Max Hurst. He is the son of President Hurst and he is here to tour this Center."

"I see."

Unlike the formality that Officer Hamby presented, Max extended his hand in a friendly manner. "Forgive me for any inconvenience, Pastor Cline. I feel almost as though I know you. I at least know all about you." Max laughed awkwardly. "I handle the statistics on all the Centers in this Sector. I manage the main frame in Greece."

"Oh, yes," he said smiling suddenly. "I understand. A couple of our young men here have been chatting with you." He gestured to a computer that was their limited connection to the outside world.

"Well, if it is a tour you want, come along; almost everyone is in the garden this morning. Those that are not in the garden are doing laundry or preparing meals. "You have seen the office," he said. "We take turns doing what little record keeping is necessary."

He led them to the middle building where most of the families slept in crowded, sparsely furnished dorm rooms. They went upstairs where there were two large rooms on either end of a long hallway. The hallway had rooms on either side. "This is where the single men sleep. The single women are at the other end of the hall. The other rooms up here are for families. The rooms were neat and extremely clean as were all the other rooms he saw.

As soon as they exited at the far end of the building, Max could hear children laughing and the low melodious hum of women talking. They walked around the side of the building and just behind the sanctuary was a grassy secluded area. "This is the laundry and shower area; as you can see, it is wash day." The women were busy washing huge tubs of laundry. Some of the younger girls were hanging freshly washed cloths. Small children romped and played as though they were on a holiday outing.

Next, Max was shown the interior of the sanctuary. It was cool and quiet inside, and the surreal light streaming in from the many stained glass windows gave Max a peculiar, peaceful feeling. "This is where we meet for worship and other meetings," Pastor Cline said. "We even house some of our 'guests' in the balcony!"

As they crossed the courtyard toward the dining room, they paused at the pool. Max put his hand into the clear liquid. "This water is as cold as ice!" he exclaimed.

"Yes. Hard to believe, isn't it?" Pastor Cline said with a smile.

They entered the dining room and proceeded to the kitchen where several women were preparing the noon meal. A huge pot of stew simmered on the old wood-burning cook stove that had been installed on the deck just outside the kitchen. Rows of dry wood were stacked close by.

"Ready to see a true miracle, gentlemen?" Pastor Cline asked as he led them out of the kitchen and into the side yard. "This is our garden. It provides nourishment for all the residents in this Center." He didn't tell them that it also was excellent barter for other "necessary" items from outside the confines of the fence, like chickens or wood for the cook stove.

Max saw men and women toiling in the lush green garden. They were intent on their work, tilling, planting, and harvesting the crops.

"Why is this such a miracle? I've seen gardens in Belgium just as lush."

"Perhaps, *but* have you ever seen one without a weed or a pest? Or have you ever seen one that produces perpetually?"

"It's easy to see how this small army could pull weeds and squash bugs," Officer Hamby laughed. "That's all they have to occupy their time!" His laughter faded as he caught a disapproving look from Max.

"We don't pull weeds in this garden. Neither do we destroy bugs. They simply do not exist here."

Max smiled now. "Pastor, do you really expect us to believe that?"

"Believe it or not," he shrugged, "it is true."

Just at that moment a dinner bell sounded and the people working in the garden began to move slowly toward them. "You will have lunch with us won't you, Mr. Hurst? We have plenty to share."

"Thank you, Pastor; as a matter of fact, I would like that very much. Would you please inform the Foster brothers that they are to dine with me? I am looking forward to meeting them in person."

Pastor Cline went to where the two young men were washing up with the others.

He brought them to where Max was waiting. "Jason, Duane, this is Mr. Hurst. He has come to tour our Center and meet you two, it seems."

"Hello, Mr. Hurst," Jason said extending his hand.

"Please. Call me Max."

"Hi, Max," Duane said, also shaking hands. "You're a lot younger than I imagined."

Max laughed and the three of them relaxed as they sat down and resumed their conversation in the same friendly manner they had used when they were chatting across the continents.

After dinner the others left to resume their various duties. Officer Hamby went to the courtyard to smoke, and the three of them were left alone in the dining hall. "You do seem to be managing extraordinarily well," Max, stated. "There is one thing though, that I would like you to clarify for me."

"And what is that?" Jason asked.

"You inferred that you were being taken care of."

"Yes?"

"You inferred that angels are taking care of you."

"We believe that."

"Have you seen angels flying around here then?"

"Yes, we have," Duane said. "Didn't you see them? We thought everyone must have seen them."

"When?"

"You know. When the warning was given about the registration number. Didn't you see them?"

"I saw something, yes. I heard the warning too, but I don't believe I saw angels. What I did see was an elaborately staged hoax! Attempts are made everyday to overthrow the new system, and we even have new information from the Russian Sector that they may be at the bottom of a conspiracy to overthrow the government. We aren't worried though. We won't be deterred."

"Your system is doomed," predicted Duane in a matter-of-fact tone.

Max looked surprised and hurt, as though he had been personally attacked. "This new system is the best thing that ever happened to this planet," Max countered, "mankind is about to reach heights never before imagined."

"That is only true because the King of Kings is about to return and claim His Kingdom," Duane announced boldly.

Max shook his head. It was time to leave. He had seen and heard enough to know that he was dealing with hard-nosed fundamentalists who were sitting around waiting for pie in the sky.

"These dissidents have it pretty good," Officer Hamby observed as they left the Confinement Center. "Better than most people on the outside in a lot of ways."

"We have our freedom," Max reminded him.

"Do we?" Hamby asked, thinking about all the people that had been forced to return to their countries of origin. "Is relocation freedom?"

"Don't knock it. The system is working."

After careful consideration of his son's report upon his return, President Hurst had agreed with Officer Hamby. The dissidents had it too good. The screw must be turned. Maxwell sent out an order that brought about a persecution that even he was sorry he had unleashed.

Chapter 35

"Dad, I don't think you have any idea what kind of havoc your 'Participation Law' is causing!" Max had arrived in Brussels from Villa Rose that morning to attend a party in Leslie's honor and to be fitted for his tuxedo.

"Perhaps not, but I *do* know one thing, it is working to bring more people into subjection every day."

"I can *not* believe you can sit here and condone the tactics that are being used by the Regional Commanders," Max argued. "Especially when you know the extremes they are going to in order to line their own coffers with the bounty they get for each registration. The atrocities range from beatings and rape to outright blatant torture!"

"I think you are over-reacting, Max. Sure, there have been a *few* cases of abuse, I won't deny that, but it isn't as widespread as you make it sound."

"Dad, it is bad, believe me. In any case, *one* incident of torture would be one incident too many. Our society can't be built on that!"

"Our society is *not* built on that!" Maxwell said, emphatically. "Max, why don't you look around and see all the good this new society has brought about. Do you see any starving babies in the African Sector or in India? Do you see any families without a roof over their heads? Do you see masses of people out of work? Or hungry? Or thirsty for pure water?"

Maxwell angrily threw Max's report on the table. "Just keep your nose out of it, Son!" Just do your job and keep your damn nose out of it!"

Max turned and walked out. He knew it was useless to argue, his father had become dogmatic and beyond reason. He went back to Villa Rose, cut off his relationships with any individuals in the Centers, threw himself into his work, and buried his head in the sand. He didn't see his father again until just before the wedding and when he did see him the subject was never mentioned.

"Hot head," Maxwell muttered at the back of his retreating son.

"Why was Max in such a hurry to leave Belgium this afternoon?" Marion asked at dinner. "He could have spent the night, at least."

Maxwell was relieved that Max hadn't told his mother about their discussion. He *would* have his hands full if Marion knew everything that was going on.

"Guess he has a lot of work to get caught up on before he meets us in Rome."

"He seemed upset about something."

"Marion. Drop it. Everything is all right."

Maxwell's stern tone disturbed Marion and she knew the subject *must* be dropped.

"Sweetheart!" Maxwell turned to his daughter to further distance himself from any discussion with Marion. "Fill me in on the happenings."

Leslie smiled brightly. "Paul and I have met with Jeff. He likes the service we have planned. He says it is simple and simply beautiful!"

"I told you he would like it, didn't I?"

"Yes, Dad you did."

"Leslie and I are going to Rome the first of the week," Marion said. "We are meeting with the wedding director one last time."

"Isn't it exciting? I'll soon be *Mrs. Paul Roberts*!"

Maxwell laughed approvingly while Marion hid her true feelings behind a demure little smile. For the most part she was happy for her exuberant daughter.

This wedding was going to rival any State Affair past, present, or future. Invitations had been sent to everyone of any importance in the entire world it seemed. They, along with friends and relatives, would surely fill the great vault of Saint Peter's Cathedral. The citizens of Rome would fill the square, and the entire population of the world would be in attendance via their Net Connections.

Over the years Vatican City with Saint Peter's had become an international symbol of the ecumenical movement: a shrine that had solidified them into one Universal Church. Now as the true fulfillment of the movement was about to be realized, even this glorious city would be forced to yield to the most glorious city of all, and the Basilica would pale before the splendor of the new Temple in Jerusalem. But for now, the pageantry of the coming event would transpire within the cloistered, protective walls of Vatican City and under the watchful eyes of the famous Swiss Guards who would attend all the festivities, including the reception that would be held in the Palace.

Marion and Leslie had arrived at the Vatican Villa early in the week and had been warmly received by the Bishop of Rome. Jeff was there and the day had been spent going over details of the ceremony and the security that was necessary.

Jeff and the Bishop had retired early, and Leslie and her mother were in their suite curled up on a plush sofa going over the events of the day.

"Those Swiss Guards make me jittery! They remind me of giant bees, buzzing around in their gold and yellow striped uniforms!"

Marion laughed. "They are merely a part of the wedding package, darling. This is probably the safest place on earth to have a wedding of this magnitude."

Leslie sipped her wine slowly, not speaking for long minutes. "Mom?" she said in a near whisper. "What's it like?"

"What, dear?"

"I don't know what it is like. Do you know what I mean?" Leslie could not lift her head to look into her Mother's eyes. "I'm still a virgin."

Marion moved closer and took her daughter into her arms lifting her head until the two women were face to face. There was a long silence. "My darling daughter, Paul is the most gentle and compassionate man I have ever known, and believe me, it will be the most precious experience of your life to become one with him."

"Thank you, Mommy," Leslie murmured with the reassured acceptance of a child. "Thank you."

The next few days were filled with last minute duties. People trailed in and out of the Villa in gay parades. The family began arriving from the United States. The attendants of the bride and groom came from around the world, and at last the groom himself.

Finally, Maxwell came from Brussels to complete the wedding party.

The wedding day was glorious and sun filled. Maxwell and Leslie were driven from the Villa to Saint Peter's Square in a horse drawn coach. The Swiss Guard standing shoulder to shoulder formed a secure avenue between the adoring throngs of people who crowded the square and had come as much to see their President as his beautiful daughter. The progress of the carriage was accompanied by thunderous applause and shouts. Maxwell waved his greetings and the now familiar fullness swelled in his chest. He pulled Leslie closer and at that moment felt like a triumphant gladiator in a magnificent coliseum.

When the horses stopped, Maxwell took Leslie's hand and helped her from the carriage and they moved up the esplanade to the doors of the cathedral. Maxwell turned to face the crowd of cheering well wishers. He lifted his arms in a majestic stance and an immediate and deep hush fell. The doors swung open and he and Leslie disappeared into the great narthex. There they met the wedding director and the rest of the bridal attendants. Maxwell took his daughter into his arms for a final hug then pushed her out at arms length to look at her. "You are a vision of beauty," he proclaimed as her maid-of-honor arranged her veil and straightened the train on her wedding dress.

From somewhere deep inside the Basilica, a wedding march rang out inviting them to enter and begin the long ceremonious march up the beautiful marble nave between the isles filled with dignitaries and guests. Gigantic stone figures lined the walls looking down on the proceedings in cold silence. The echo of their footsteps and the swishing sound of voluminous garments were swallowed in the swell of music, as it seemed to thunder in the veins of the wedding party.

To Leslie it seemed an eternity passed before she was able to join Paul beneath the immense bronze canopy that covered the altar. Jeff, robed in rich priestly garments, looked down at them smiling with pleasure. Maxwell stood between them and an understanding look passed between the two men as Maxwell gave his daughter into the hands of his life long friend and stepped back to join his own wife.

As the service proceeded, details blurred together in a kaleidoscope of sights and sounds that seemed to echo from somewhere deep in the very bowels of St. Peter's, as though the Cathedral had taken on a life of its own. Then she was being kissed with warmth and feeling that flooded her very being and brought all the fractured sensations into brilliant focus. She was Mrs. Paul Luther Roberts at last.

Later that afternoon, after the formal pictures had been taken, the entire wedding party went into seclusion to rest before the banquet and ball that was scheduled for that evening.

The groomsman and the maid-of-honor had carefully put away the wedding clothes and left the newly weds alone at last. Leslie came willingly into his waiting arms, and Paul kissed her lips and caressed her body in ways that took her to heights she had never imagined. Then just as she was ready to enter into some oblivious, joyful state of ecstasy he began to pull himself, and her, back to reality, relaxing little by little until every muscle in his body was again under his control. The pleading look in her eyes was silenced as he placed his finger lightly on her lips.

"Remember our vow?" he asked. " The vow we made at Sand Beach?"

"Yes," she whispered heavily, not at all as committed to their pledge as he seemed to be.

"It is only one more day. I promise you, my love, it will be worth the wait." He cupped her delicate, beautiful face in his hands and kissed her tenderly.

They flew to Maine the following morning to begin their honeymoon and when they finally arrived at Sand Beach, Leslie discovered that Paul truly was a man of his word!

CHAPTER 36

Maxwell stood in the Court of Priests. The massive, highly polished, bronze altar with its four ornate horns was now complete. Goldsmiths were at that very moment overlaying the exterior of the sanctuary in thin layers of the precious metal. The light tapping of their tools reverberated in his ears like the pounding of his own heart each time he stood in this place. There were other sounds in the background creating a constant din. The thunder of jackhammers, the roar of heavy equipment, the shouts of supervisors trying to make themselves heard over the noise, all seemed to dance together in a daily rhythm, accompanied by loud music blasting from a nearby radio.

"Oh! *Here* you are!" Jeff said, as though he had searched the entire area. "I should have known I would find you here. When I want to find *you* I look in the Temple. When I want to find *Marion* I look in the Palace!"

Maxwell laughed because it was true. "Isn't this just breathtaking, Jeff? They *are* on schedule? Right?"

"Don't worry. Everything will be completed well before Word Day," Jeff said reassuringly. "Let's go have lunch. Have you forgotten that Marion is joining us?"

Maxwell glanced at his watch. Time stopped for him, whenever he entered this holy realm. Here he felt a power that was timeless and each time he came it was more difficult to pull himself away.

Marion had even commented on it after their last visit. "Each time we return from Jerusalem, I feel you leave a piece of yourself there," she had said.

He left with Jeff, glancing back at the shrouded inner sanctum, and he knew there would come a day when he would never have to leave. "Sorry we're late, darling," Maxwell apologized as they approached the table where Marion waited. The restaurant was on the top floor of an exclusive hotel, and from here one could survey the entire city of Jerusalem including the Temple site and the Palace just behind it.

"Couldn't tear yourself away again?" The sarcasm was meant to be humorous, but a hint of resentment could be detected in her tone.

"That's right," Maxwell confessed. "I couldn't tear myself away but for your sake I was rescued. Jeff tore me away," he replied, mocking her testy humor.

"Ta, Ta, we are all here now. Let's eat. I'm famished!" Jeff announced changing the mood as quickly as a talented choir director changes the tempo of his music.

"How are Paul and Leslie doing? Ecstatic I imagine."

"Yes. Very," Marion replied, "but not as ecstatic as the prospective grandfather I suspect. Maxwell was beside himself when they told us."

Maxwell broke into a big grin. The anticipation of being a grandparent temporarily superseded his thought of the Temple. "You should see Leslie, Jeff!" He held his hand out in front of his middle, "She's got a little ball. Right here in front! If you put your hand on it or watch real close, every once in a while the little guy will roll around in there and you can actually see it. It's incredible!"

"I'm sure it is," Jeff laughed, "I'll take your word for it." Jeff had never married. Although there was a possibility he may have sired children, he could not identify with the experience of pregnancy. "Is Max excited about becoming an uncle?"

Marion appeared distressed at the mention of her son. "We see very little of Max these days," she said sadly, "he chooses to bury himself in his work at Villa Rose. He won't socialize. He does his job and that's about it."

Maxwell shot Jeff a warning glance. The two men had discussed concern for Max's mental state earlier, but he had not confided anything to Marion. "Max has a big job. That's all. *And* he is very dedicated."

Max had returned to Thera after the wedding intending to keep his mind exclusively on the Sectors assigned to him, however, it wasn't long before he discovered the wide spread use of brutality practiced by the Regional Commanders. Unregistered citizens were executed outright when they were caught outside their Centers. Dissidents were venturing out more and more, boldly preaching a coming salvation when *anyone* who would listen and accept their "Jesus" would be evacuated from the planet. Max gradually began to recede into a severe depression.

Jeff had suggested that Maxwell 'get him a girl'. "How would you have survived all those years without Carmen? Just send him a Carmen." Maxwell had tried Jeff's suggestion but even a beautiful woman had failed to interest Max. Max is Max, his father had finally stated, closing the matter. The two men had not spoken of it again.

"Seen any *overseers* lately, Jeff?" Maxwell asked, heading off any more discussion of Max. The overseers, as they had come to be known, were the objects that were seen occasionally hovering in the sky above the Temple site. The objects were unaffected by laser fire and it was impossible to try anything else for fear of damage to the area below.

"Not lately, but I have this weird feeling that they are there whether we can see them or not."

"That's a cockeyed notion, Jeff. Are you suggesting they are supernatural or something?"

"No. Not really. It's just a feeling I get."

Marion laughed, "Well, it's a good thing we don't live our lives according to our *feelings*! Maxwell would still be standing in the Temple gazing up at god knows what!"

"So you *do* still see them?" Maxwell asked again, ignoring Marion's remark.

"Occasionally."

"The most recent sighting was over a Control Center in Africa," Maxwell said. "The Ministry of Defense moved in with every weapon known to man. We threw everything we had at it. Nothing!" Maxwell didn't tell Jeff in front of Marion that although the efforts had failed to damage the target that hovered over the Center, the Center and everyone in it had been destroyed. The craft had disappeared and was not seen at that site again.

"Have they found anything in the Russian Sector?"

"So far, nothing. I know we are getting close, though, I can just feel it."

"No feelings. Remember?"

"That's right," Maxwell laughed. "We'll have a breakthrough soon. I'd like to crack this case before World Day."

"You haven't got much time then," Jeff said, pushing back his chair. "Speaking of time, I've got a meeting with the "Big Three" this afternoon. We have a few kinks to iron out if we want everything to come together for your inauguration on World Day." Jeff pushed his chair back and stood up, "You're going back to Brussels this afternoon?"

"Yes, the baby is due any day and we wouldn't miss that for the world!" Maxwell gave it a second thought. "Well, maybe for *World Day*," he smiled, knowingly.

"Sure you would," Marion said, getting up. She was just as anxious for World Day to arrive, although she wouldn't reveal that the thought of living in the Palace on the Temple grounds nearly consumed her every waking moment and when she slept she dreamed of it.

Maxwell and Marion gazed down as the Hovercraft circled high over the city of Jerusalem. Each saw a vision: one a golden Temple with the lust of his heart, the other a golden Palace with the lust of her eye. Each was totally captivated.

Chapter 37

Maxwell reached, groggily for the phone. "Yes, Paul? What's wrong?" Maxwell listened quietly then he asked, "Is Leslie all right?" Marion, who had also been awakened, tensed, sensing that something had gone wrong. "We will be there as soon as we can, hang in there, Paul." He hung up the phone and turned to Marion, "Leslie had the baby. A little boy. There are some problems."

"With Leslie?" Marion asked with mounting fear.

"No. The baby."

Maxwell called the chauffeur and then the two of them dressed hurriedly. "Damn his hide to hell, I don't know why Paul didn't call me before they left for the hospital," Maxwell muttered as he shoved his wallet into his back pocket.

"Leslie didn't want us there until after the baby came. She was *very* emphatic about that."

"I know she didn't, but Paul knew what *I* wanted. I had made myself *very* clear," Maxwell said tersely.

The trip into town seemed to take forever. They held hands as they huddled together in the limo enduring the time in silence. The sun was beginning to rise as they reached the Regional Medical Center where escorts were waiting to take them to the maternity complex.

Paul was in a private waiting room when they arrived. He was unaware of their presence as he sat with his head cradled in his hands, sobbing uncontrollably. Marion placed her hand on his shoulder and he looked up at her. "The baby," he whispered. Maxwell spun around and quickly left the room. Marion dropped to her knees beside Paul and gathered him into her arms, joining her tears to his. Paul clung to her in desperation as she soothed and caressed him with all the tenderness that was in her aching heart.

Maxwell went to the top of the building where he stood alone, cursing the heavens. He bellowed and howled like a madman. No tears came, only this deep mysterious anger that somehow could only be expressed in a fit of uncontrollable rage. There was no help for him except time. Indeed, if Marion or anyone else had attempted to approach him he may have done something unthinkable. In time the hour of railing ended. He went back to the waiting room to face the hard part. Leslie would have to be told. They were waiting quietly for him and when he arrived, Marion went to her husband as much for comfort as to comfort him, but when she embraced him she felt a coldness that sent a chill to her very heart.

The loss of her baby sent Leslie into a deep depression that no one seemed able to penetrate. Maxwell spent most of his time in Jerusalem preparing for World Day. When he wasn't there, he was somewhere else in the world polishing his image.

Paul brought Leslie back to Gasbeek where Marion could keep a tender, doting eye on her daughter. The move was only a little premature since Paul and Leslie had planned to occupy the castle when Maxwell and Marion moved to Jerusalem.

"Why don't I take Leslie to Acadia," Paul asked Marion one morning as they were eating breakfast. Leslie was in her room as usual. "Do you think that might help? God knows I have tried everything else I can think of!"

"I think that is a marvelous idea, Paul. Leslie loves Acadia. She has wonderful childhood memories of the place."

Marion hoped her enthusiasm for the idea was not too obvious. She was more than anxious to get back to Jerusalem to personally supervise the furnishing of the Palace, and if Paul took Leslie to Acadia, she could also leave Brussels.

Paul smiled with delight and thought to himself, "Yes, Leslie does have beautiful memories of Acadia and I am a big part of those memories!"

"Excuse me, Marion," he said, "I am going to discuss this with Leslie right away."

Leslie had gratefully agreed to the trip. Maxwell had returned to Belgium to see them off. It looked as though things would finally get back to normal. "Try to enjoy yourself, Leslie," Maxwell said. "It isn't fair to Paul if you carry on with this grieving thing forever. We all have to go on with our lives sooner or later." He hugged her before giving her a stern reminder. "Now remember. You *must* be in Jerusalem next month for World Day. Come hell or high water you are going to be there! So get with it, girl, I want you fit and sassy." He gave her a little pat on her bottom as he pushed her toward the boarding gate and back into the future.

"You'll have to be more convincing than that to get Max to come to Jerusalem," Marion said as they prepared to board their own jet.

"He'll come willingly or I'll drag him!"

"He wouldn't even come to the baby's funeral," Marion reminded him.

"He'll come," Maxwell growled.

There was so much to do to get ready for World Day that the two of them hardly saw each other during the next month. Marion was deeply involved with decorators, curators, chefs, and domestic staff preparing for the first official state affair that would follow the inauguration of World Day. She was determined to make it the most elaborate coming out that history had ever recorded. After all, they would be celebrating the third and final phase of the plan that would herald an era of lasting peace and prosperity for all mankind. The Church and State united at last and her own husband at the helm!

Chapter 38

Acadia had been the cure for Leslie. She gradually blossomed back into her old self. She and Paul had even spent a weekend at Sand Beach where Paul had welcomed her back into his arms as though hailing one back from the grave.

After that their days were filled with adventure as they re-discovered the Island and each other. "I'd like to go to the Exchange in Bar Harbor today," Leslie announced one particularly beautiful, sunny morning as they finished breakfast. The Atlantic Ocean stretched out below them like a magnificent emerald jewel.

"What on earth for?" Paul asked.

"I don't know. Perhaps I'm just curious. It has been ages since I have been allowed to browse and shop on my own." When the domestics didn't do the shopping Leslie ordered over the Net. "Perhaps I just want to rub elbows with the locals and find out how it would be to just be good old common folk!"

"What ever makes *you* happy, my darling, wife. I'm game."

"Can you borrow Jake's pick up? I want to go incognito."

"Just what are you up to?" Paul asked, getting a little suspicious. "What have you got up your sleeve?"

"Nothing! I just don't want to be the President's daughter today, that's all," she said as she left the room to go and get dressed.

Paul, who always dressed before breakfast, read the morning paper while he waited.

'*Preparations for World Day Underway*', was the headline, 'Plans are nearly complete for the inauguration of World Day set to take place in Jerusalem this month. Dignitaries from every Nation State will attend the formal transfer of power from Brussels to Jerusalem when the Temple is dedicated on June 30, bringing to fruition the dream of a United World. President Hurst revealed in a recent interview that the union of the three ecclesiastical streams was a direct result of the ingenious efforts of Archbishop Richards. President Hurst further stated that the historic union of Jews, Muslims, and Christians is the last vital link to completing the third and final phase of the plan to solidify the United States of the World.'

Paul scanned the paper to discover a second, provocative headline couched in the form of a question. '*Where Will You Be On World Day*? Some of you will be lucky enough to be in the courts of the Temple in Jerusalem either in an official capacity or as a guest who has earned the right of pilgrimage. In any case all the Nation States in the world are obligated to attend this historic event. But whether you are in Jerusalem or attending in your own Regional Temple, you must attend! Every able-bodied man, woman, and child is required to attend the inauguration. The only exceptions are for the extremely ill or elderly confined to Medical Centers. Your Temple Priest will continue to provide updated information.'

A final bit of news caught his attention, '*Dissident Activity Intensifies*. As World Day approaches it seems there has been an increase in infractions of the Confinement Law by dissidents around the globe. Their boldness is earning them instant rewards; in some Sectors they are disposed of on the spot. These enemies of our system spout a message of salvation from the *wicked world doomed to wrath* from which they alone shall be spared. They look to the heavens for the coming of a *King of Kings* as their propaganda claims.'

"What garbage," Paul thought.

Leslie re-appeared in a pair of tight fitting blue jeans and a loose comfortable sweater. "I can't believe I can still get into these pants," she laughed.

Paul put down the paper and looked at his petite wife. "We can't go anywhere together like *this*!" He stood up and gestured to his own immaculate, tailored appearance. "I must admit though. *You* look pretty darn cute!"

"Don't just stand there grinning at me! Go upstairs and change. I've borrowed more than wheels from Jake!"

"Why, you conniving little wench!" he teased, "I believe you *do* intend to have a good time!"

When they climbed into Jake's truck, they *did* look like a couple of ordinary people, in spite of Paul's baggy jeans. Leslie sat close to Paul and they sang old country songs as the truck bounced along the twisted mountain road toward the city.

The citizens of Bar Harbor had long been about the business of the day. There were a few truck farms in the area but the main industry was fishing. The population here, as in every Region, had been regulated by relocation to ensure jobs for all. Therefore, this whole area had the aura of a lazy little fishing village where every body knew everybody else and strangers were usually regarded with suspicion. It wasn't surprising that a Control Car pulled up behind Jake's pickup as soon as Paul stopped in front of the Exchange.

A Control Officer got out and came to the driver's side eyeing Paul with caution, "State your registration number, article number one, fifteen, and twenty of the WORD."

Paul grinned as he rattled off his ID number then went on to say, "article one states: 'Strict obedience to the articles of the WORD is fundamental to the System, article fifteen states: 'Stealing is a crime against the order punishable by death, and article twenty states: 'Temple instruction is mandatory and must be attended once a week by all citizens, either Friday, Saturday, or Sunday'.

The officer, who had already scanned and confirmed Paul's official identity, felt foolish and looked embarrassed. "Sorry to bother you, Mr. Roberts. Just doing my job. We don't see many strangers around here and we get credits for captured dissidents."

"That's quite all right, officer. Glad to see you doing your job. This is my wife, Mrs. Roberts."

"Pleased to meet you, Mrs. Roberts," he said politely tipping his hat, while resisting the urge to ask them what in the hell they were doing in Bar Harbor dressed like a couple of bums!

Leslie smiled. A huge, delightful childish smile. Then she said, as though in answer to his unspoken question, "We just want to look around," she said simply. "*Incognito*!"

"Be my guest. I'll radio the Control Center and make sure you aren't bothered again."

"Thanks Officer. We'd appreciate that."

Paul got out of the truck and opened Leslie's door and they went into the Exchange. The huge warehouse served the needs of the entire Region. Every item deemed necessary could be bought here, from nails to groceries. Surplus vegetables, fruits, and crafts could also be brought here to sell or exchange with other individuals who wished to participate in a limited form of free enterprise. Unnecessary luxury items were forbidden. Few people were in the Exchange this early in the day, and those who were neither spoke nor smiled. Leslie soon lost interest in strolling through rows and rows of isles filled with un-inviting, bland generic products.

"This is boring," she stated, "Let's go, Paul."

They visited the Regional Medical Center next: A facility where everything medical happened, from birthing to brain scans, ingrown toenails to open heart surgery. The waiting room was filled with people. Some were engaged in lively discussions, mothers were comforting whimpering babies, and old men sat lopsided snoozing in the midst of it all. Doctors, nurses, and other caregivers went about their business with mundane efficiency. An attitude of ho-hum-ness permeated the place, the side effect of long years of socialized medicine in an era when careers were assigned by aptitude and need instead of greed and self-gratification. The entire complex was sterile and spotless, especially the nursery. Leslie looked longingly at the newborn babies behind the glass enclosure.

"Paul, you better get me out of here before I go in there and kidnap one of them."

"We'll have one of our own," he promised, putting a comforting arm around her. "Are you hungry? Shall we get some lunch before we tour the Temple?"

"Yes, let's eat first. I'm famished."

Like all other businesses the eateries were based on a need rather than greed principal, and there were only two choices in Bar Harbor: a typical family style restaurant with a buffet of ordinary every day fare or a fast food complex with a variety of hot dogs, hamburgers and pizza. They chose the fast food and ate what tasted like cardboard pizza while wishing they had packed a lunch and brought it with them from Acadia.

"That was the worst lunch I have ever eaten," Leslie confessed as they got back into Jake's truck.

"Perhaps we should have tried the Cafeteria after all."

"Anything would have been better than that pizza!"

The Temple was situated on a quiet hill overlooking the town. It was the last stop on their sight seeing tour, and frankly, both were anxious to get back to Acadia. This was a foreign world to them, a world that didn't feel comfortable to either of them.

"Ah, this feels much better," Paul said leading Leslie into the cool interior of familiar opulence. All the Regional Temples were identical in design and function. Two sets of ornately carved double doors were set opposite each other, one to enter and one to exit. Each door was uniquely designed to roll into the curve of the Temple wall, and each opened to reveal an expansive narthex with a pair of curved stairs leading up to balconies and clerical offices. The main auditorium was an immense circular room surrounded by elaborately carved wooden columns. The intricate circular designs in the marble floor were both aesthetic and functional, providing orderly standing room for worshiping citizens. The richly paneled, curved walls behind the columns served as a background for rare paintings and other beautiful objects from many lands that filled specially designed niches creating a museum of rare art and artifacts.

On one side several doors lead out into the Priest's Quarters, where behind cloistered walls celibate men and women in scarlet robes taught the precepts of the WORD, oversaw the upkeep of the Temple, and were in charge of the immense stores of art treasures and wealth that was shared between the Regional Temples for the benefit of each citizen. On the other side, a heavily draped platform served as a podium and concealed a huge computer monitor.

Leslie walked to the center of the great assembly room and looked up at the huge overhead dome. The intricate stained glass skylight was a work of art in itself, and the sunlight filtering down upon her made her look like someone from another world. "Someone very beautiful," Paul thought as he walked toward her and pulled her into his arms. "Care to dance?" he said as he hummed an old waltz tune. As they swirled together under the multicolored glow of the skylight they reclaimed the spirit of the day. They left the Temple, got into Jack's old beat up truck, and drove back up the winding road to Acadia to resume life in their own world.

Chapter 39

Paul and Leslie flew directly to Jerusalem. It was the day before World Day. Maxwell and Marion had taken up residence in the Palace and Max was scheduled to meet them there. He had given his father little trouble about coming. Family loyalty had won over after all, and he was prepared to play the part of an obedient son.

"*Mother*! How can you even relax in all this gaudy splendor?" Leslie exclaimed as they were touring the Palace.

"*Gaudy splendor*?" Marion croaked incredulously. She had put her heart and soul into projecting a sense of glorious royalty and her own daughter had the gall to call her efforts 'gaudy splendor'.

"Never mind, Leslie," Maxwell reassured his daughter, "I make her sleep on goat hair sheets just to keep her humble." Maxwell's humor avoided a head on collision between the two women. Leslie had no way of knowing how profoundly this move had changed her mother, nor could she predict the change that was about to transform her father in the space of a day.

Jeff came sweeping into the room in his new clerical robes like a cardinal in flight. "Welcome! Welcome!" he said cheerfully, holding out his arms to receive Leslie and Max in a warm embrace. He was so full of anticipation and good humor that his mood was contagious. "Isn't this just glorious?" he asked gesturing grandly to the surroundings. "Just wait until you see the Temple tomorrow!"

Leslie glanced at her beaming mother, "I can hardly wait," she thought.

Servants, dressed in white dinner jackets, served dinner in the formal dining room. Leslie had found it a little difficult to zip her gown since she had gained a few pounds during their wonderful lazy month at Acadia. Marion and Maxwell looked absolutely majestic and all eyes were on them as they entered the huge hall.

Jeff stood in their honor and lifted his glass for the toast. The party consisted of relatives and close friends. The aged Mikeal had made the pilgrimage, certain that it would be his last. Rolph had come with Max and the two men were side by side at the table. Marion's sister and her family, Maxwell's two sisters and only surviving brother, and of course Paul and Leslie all stood holding their glasses high as they echoed Jeff's proclamation. "To our President and his Lady! To the United States of the World!"

It was a wonderful reunion and before the night was over everyone was in very high spirits. When at last they did retire, Maxwell found it very difficult to unwind. He lay awake in his bed long after everyone else had fallen asleep.

Sometime during the night Maxwell slipped out of his bed and went out on the balcony. The full moon hung luminous and golden in a clear night sky. The Temple to the east of the Palace could be seen shimmering gloriously in the bright moonlight. The warm glow that seemed to emanate from it enlarged and expanded until Maxwell felt himself bathed in its splendor and engulfed in a trance like peace. He closed his eyes and lifted his face to the heavens. Waves of celestial rapture flooded his being as the full anointing was poured out upon his flesh. He had no idea how long he had stood entranced in the moonlight, but when he finally did return to his bed he fell instantly into a deep sleep and dreamt the dreams of the gods.

CHAPTER 40

Maxwell awoke to the rumble of thunder and the drumming of a pouring rain. He got out of bed, pulled the glass doors together, and stood looking out on the drenched city with disappointment.

"This may blow over," he thought, "but if it doesn't this is one parade that will not be called off because of inclement weather!"

Marion was in the dressing room. She had slept peacefully and looked refreshed. "Good morning, darling," she greeted her husband cheerfully. "Sleep well?" she asked as though this were just any ordinary day.

"Yes. Thank you," he said, resisting the temptation to share his vision with her. Instead he headed for the shower. They were scheduled to have Brunch with the Commissioners before the inauguration that was set to take place at noon. Maxwell, knowing the magnitude of the occasion, was already nervous as a cat.

It was useless to try and eat and even more difficult to carry on useless conversation. The tension mounting in Maxwell was almost static and as soon as the meal was over he excused himself to seek a secluded place where he could pull himself together. He went out on the portico facing the Temple. The rain was still coming down steadily. He had the sensation that he was not alone and the tiny hairs on the back of his neck attested to the fact. He closed his eyes and instantly was flooded with a warm sense of peace. He was reminded of Her promise to always be with him and his courage was renewed.

He opened his eyes just in time to see the clouds recede and the sun burst forth as a day reborn. Throngs of people already filled the various courts beginning with the Court of Priests where the Commissioners and other dignitaries were standing. In the outer court umbrellas were folded as the huge crowd of people welcomed the sudden appearance of a brilliant sun. Wisps of steam shimmered heavenward from the cool marble pavement.

Jeff, in his flowing scarlet robe, met Maxwell on the walkway above the colonnade. The two men embraced.

"This is it, Jeff. The *big* day. *World Day!*"

"We've worked hard for this Maxwell, I just hope we're ready."

"We're ready, old friend."

The two men walked to the elevator that took them down to the lowest level beneath the Temple. After a short walk they entered a second elevator that took them up to the Inner Sanctum of the Temple. Maxwell immediately took his place in the Holy of Holies behind the royal blue velvet curtain. Jeff would take his place in the Sanctuary behind ornately carved sliding doors that at the proper time would open to the Court of Priests. Jeff was prepared to open the World Day Inauguration with a short speech about the importance of strict, timely obedience. The ceremony was to be sent live where people gathered in Temples all around the world.

"It's time, Maxwell. Are you ready? No turning back now."

Maxwell felt a twinge in the pit of his stomach; he took a deep breath and said, "I'm ready."

The dimly lit thirty foot square room was unfurnished except for the elaborate solid gold throne flanked on either side by golden sphinx, their wings arched to form a canopy over the elevated chair of state. The walls were overlaid with embossed gold etched with an intricate design. Maxwell ascended the four steps up to the throne and sat down.

It was noon. Suddenly the earsplitting sound of a shophar was heard around the world. It was the high steady note calling all citizens of the Nation States to worship. With this ancient signal World Day was officially declared.

Cedar panels slid open and Archbishop Richards stepped forward in all his Priestly splendor. He turned to face the heavily shrouded Holy of Holies and lifting his arms toward heaven, he prayed, "Great God of the Earth, hear our prayer. Grant us peace this day. This great day of the world. Oh, God of the Earth, bless the United States of the World and our leader, President Maxwell Hurst. Amen."

He turned toward the dignitaries that filled the immediate court, but he addressed the entire world as digital cameras captured every detail and sent them spinning into space.

"I commend you this day for your obedience. You are here for a momentous occasion. I speak to all of you here in this place and all of you out there gathered in your own Regional Temples. Your obedience will be rewarded, but let me assure you, your *disobedience* will also win you instant reward," he promised sternly.

They were then treated to a virtual tour of the Temple and the Temple grounds, bringing them back to the Sanctuary where Archbishop Richards stood before the Holy of Holies. He raised his arms toward heaven. A hush fell over the land; seconds passed as the silent multitudes realized that something of great significance was about to happen.

The curtains parted and Jeff cried in a loud commanding voice, "Hear, oh hear, all people of the world. The Lord is in his Holy Temple."

As Maxwell stood to his feet a glowing pale blue light could be seen directly behind him. It grew until the iridescent image of a beautiful woman loomed above the throne, hands outstretched in an adoring gesture. "This is my beloved son," she said in a rich, velvety voice. "Hear him."

Jeff fell to his knees and placed his forehead on the floor in homage as he cried out in a loud, commanding voice, "The Lord is in his Holy Temple. Let all the earth bow down before him!"

The first family was in the front row with the Commissioners. Everyone went down as though struck by lightening, with a low rumble that sounded like distant thunder. However, one man stood straight up among the prostrate crowd. One man dared to dissent.

Maxwell gasped in disbelief, then his mouth opened wide in a silent scream that resounded into eternity, "Maxxx! Noooo!"

Nothing could save him. The silent deadly lasers shot out from all directions, severing head from body in an immediate bloodless execution.

Marion screamed in terror as Max's lifeless body crumpled beside her. The Temple began to tremble, then shake violently as somebody yelled, "earthquake!" Blind panic propelled her up and forward as she ran with Paul and Leslie up the steps to join Jeff and Maxwell. The elevator was inoperative so they fled down the stairs. Marion was sobbing uncontrollably and had to be pulled along like a rag doll. They came up again into the Palace Grounds. "Come on," shouted Paul with Leslie in tow. "We have to get air-born." They ran to the landing pad and Paul opened the door to the hovercraft and hastily pushed the others inside just as the ground began to swell beneath his feet. He jumped in and the craft lifted gently from the pad just as the concrete gave way beneath it.

Marion sat with glazed eyes staring straight ahead. Leslie was weeping in fear. Jeff and Maxwell stared at each other in disbelief. As they swept higher and higher the city below them began to crumble.

"Son-of-a-bitch! Will you look at that!" croaked Paul pointing to the North. The earth was literally cracking up from the stress of the quake, coming apart in great wrenching tears. A wall of water was beginning to build on the Mediterranean end of the fissure, sending a flood of tremendous proportions crashing into the valley, burying towns and villages in its wake. At the same time another great wall of water was coursing its way from the Red Sea in the South on a collision course in the Judean Valley, two great cymbals in one mighty clash.

Paul was frantically shouting warnings into the radio to stations below. "Evacuate the valley. Get to the highest point as quickly as possible. Flood is coming!"

Maxwell looked down in dismay as the devastating water moved relentlessly, marching like a great army swallowing up the land. His mind flashed back to the early part of the day. He reflected on the triumph and glory that this day had promised. Now he looked over at his mindless wife. He thought about his son and his breast filled with painful rage as he muttered, "The god-damn fanatical Christians had gotten to him after all!"

CHAPTER 41

The earthquake that struck the Middle East on World Day was the worst in recorded history. It lasted for seven terrifying days, rocking the entire world with the horror of its death throws. Millions lost their lives and the geography of the Holy Land was altered forever.

The city of Jerusalem, perched on a hilltop at the edge of what had become a large body of water, was heavily damaged along with the Temple and Palace. Crisis Corps from every Nation State rallied to help in the relief efforts that were underway in Israel.

Marion had been committed to a rest home and Max's body had been found and buried. The remainder of the family tried to piece together the strands of their lives like the rest of the survivors.

Christians, calling for repentance, were coming out of Confinement Centers all around the world to literally shout messages of divine judgment. Maxwell had put out a decree that any Christians on the loose would be executed on the spot. The system was sure and swift.

A larger threat came from reports that a plot was underway to overthrow the system. Rebels were on the move in remote areas of Russia and China.

"How dangerous can they be?" Maxwell asked the Minister of Defense. "They certainly can't have any supplies."

"We don't know what they have. They are so cunning we can't even locate them. They move in and out of an area faster than a weasel."

"Do they have air power?"

"A few hovercraft, other than that we aren't sure."

"What do you mean, we aren't sure?" Maxwell demanded angrily

The Minister of Defense looked around at the rest of his committee members.

"The Orbs we saw three years ago?" he paused, "they have been sighted."

"Sighted? Where?"

The Defense Minister turned on the monitor and pointed out some bright objects in the heavens. "They are approaching earth in the exact same pattern as they did the last time. We have reason to believe they are manned Space Stations.

"Russian?"

"That we don't know."

"What about the new weapon system? Is it ready?"

The Minister looked distressed. "No, sir, it is not quite ready. It lacks about six months to completion."

"Six months?" Maxwell shouted, "what have you been dragging your asses on? This was top priority!"

"There have been unavoidable delays. We are working around the clock."

"Perfect timing," Maxwell thought, "I'm up to my ears in a local crisis and the Commies launch an offensive to overthrow the government."

It seemed that everything came to a standstill for the next few stressful days as a world of people watched the Orbs descend on their world for a second time in a little over three years. They were gripped in the destructive vice of fear, wondering about their fate. Then, just as the last time, when it seemed a collision with earth was inevitable they stopped suddenly, hovering in space high overhead.

Maxwell ordered that all the modern weaponry in the arsenal be used to try and penetrate the invisible shield that surround the unidentified craft. His men and fighter jets were lost one after another as they tried crashing through. Ground fire was useless. Missiles were reflected back to incur destruction on the very forces that sent them hurling into space.

Maxwell stood watching from a Palace balcony. The Orbs were beautiful as they shimmered above the city in the bright moonlight. He felt a loneliness more intense than he had experienced in his entire life. Max was dead, Marion had lost her senses, and Leslie and Paul were at Gasbeek. Then a voice from somewhere deep within his soul whispered, "You have me, Maxwell." Peals of laughter, hers or his, he couldn't tell, shook his body with a rhythm and force that sent waves of ecstasy flooding through his being. When he came to his senses he was lying on his back on the cool marble floor. He opened his eyes and looked up, half expecting the Orbs to be gone, but to his surprise they had begun to descend slowly toward the earth.

Suddenly a deep darkness fell upon the land. The moon was gone. The stars seemed to tumble from their lofty appointments like sparks in the wind. In other parts of the world, it seemed the sun was draped in black velvet.

Maxwell's terror intensified as the building began to shake and sway, "Oh, my god, another earthquake!" he thought scrambling to his feet. In total darkness he somehow found his way out of the Palace and into the garden. The black silence was broken by a distant sound that got louder and louder, crescendoing to such an ear splitting pitch that Maxwell had to cover his ears with his hands.

At the same moment a burst of light split the darkness from east to west and north to south, revealing to every living being on the face of the earth a brilliant, perfectly formed cross. An agonizing wail rose up from the city of Jerusalem and Maxwell realized that he was not alone. The apparition was gone as quickly as it had appeared, leaving a darkness so complete as to isolate every human being on the face of the earth.

Then a glorious burst of color assaulted his eyes and the huge Orbs again became visible, only now they had moved even closer and the portals on the underside of one hovering over the city of Jerusalem was clearly distinguishable. Then, as in the last encounter, the portals slowly slid open. Unlike the small one-man crafts three years ago, these ships were enormous as they moved out in silent, determined formation. Maxwell knew instinctively that a landing was intended.

His mind turned toward Marion, and suddenly he wanted to be with her. He ran to the garage where the chauffeur was trying without success to start the limousine. "Nothing electrical will work, sir."

Some uncontrollable driving force pushed him toward the street and he was running down the hill toward the rest home where Marion was hospitalized. He could hear her screaming when he entered the small compound. "My god, what's happening to her," he thought as he raced toward her room. She was tied to her bed and several attendants were trying to calm her.

"What in hell is going on here?" he thundered, pushing an orderly so hard that he fell back against the wall. Maxwell tore at the restraints as the nurse tried to utter a reason. "Mrs. Hurst insists that she must go to the Confinement Center. She says her son is there."

Maxwell gathered his wife in his arms and lifted her frail body easily off the bed. She clung to his neck, "Maxwell! It's Max. I must go to him. I must! Maxwell, please. Take me to him," she pleaded.

"Where is he, dearest?" Maxwell asked trying to humor her rather than reason with her. After all, she hadn't seen Max's cold headless body as he had.

"He's on that thing, that *thing*, take me to him. *Please*, Maxwell."

He stood Marion on her feet. "Can you walk, dearest?" he asked tenderly.

"Yes, I can walk," she answered, relieved that Maxwell was going to go with her.

"All right, then let's go." He took her hand and the two of them walked slowly out into the moonlight. Out of the city gates and toward the Confinement Center.

The glistening slivery craft was hovering close to the ground in a field near the Center. A ramp was visible, extending from the underside, and a steady stream of people in an almost trance like state were moving into the belly of the great ship as though propelled by some determined, mysterious purpose.

Marion pulled free from Maxwell's clasp and ran toward the ship. "Max!" she screamed, "Max, wait for me!"

"Marion, come back!" Maxwell shouted. He saw the ramp begin to recede into the portal and he knew she would never get there in time. She was directly under the craft when, in a surge of power, it lifted up from the earth. The force pushed her onto her back and Marion lay gazing up as the ship rose swiftly up and disappeared into the Orb. Maxwell ran to where his wife lay senseless on the ground. He gathered her into his arms and held her close as he shook his fist toward the heavens. "I'll get you for this," he screamed hoarsely, "*I'll get you for this!*"

CHAPTER 42

The events of the past days had shaken the world to the core. Every Confinement Center had been evacuated in one short hour. Who took them? Where were they taken to and why? These and a hundred other questions remained to be answered, but first the dead must be buried and last good-byes said.

Leslie was in a state of shock. She had stayed in Jerusalem for over a month after Max's death and in all that time her mother had not acknowledged her presence. Paul had begged her to come back to Brussels if only for a week and she knew she needed the comfort and love that only Paul could give her. Her father had become so distant that it frightened her to even be around him, and she secretly suspected that he, like her mother, had lost his senses. Now, standing beside him as he stood sentinel over Marion's useless body, Leslie felt a coldness emanate from him like the chill of death itself, turning him into a piece of unyielding stone. Even Jeff had failed to break through the shell that Maxwell was weaving tighter and tighter around himself.

"As soon as our meeting is over, I'm taking Leslie back to Gasbeek," Paul told Maxwell.

"Fine. That's the best thing for her," Maxwell agreed without emotion as they walked beneath the colonnade that circumferenced the Outer Court. The Council Chamber adjoining the Temple had suffered minor damage from the earthquake that had shaken the city of Jerusalem the previous month, and repairs to the Temple itself were nearly completed. The System seemed besieged with one crisis after another for which the antidote prescribed was good old-fashioned hard work.

The subject of several million people being whished off the face of the earth was hard to broach. No one could quite decide whose jurisdiction the problem fell under. At last the Department of Defense under the Peacekeeping Ministry was assigned the responsibility of the investigation.

Maxwell stood at a podium looking down at the Council of Ministers who sat in a semi circle at shiny mahogany desks. "Is the Minister of Defense ready to report?" he asked.

A tall man stood to his feet. "I am, sir." A copy of the report appeared on each desktop monitor simultaneously as well as the wall sized monitor behind Maxwell. "Our investigation reveals that on the above date a celestial phenomenon occurred that appeared to affect the entire world. We have no records of anything of this nature happening at any other time in recorded history. In conjunction with the afore-mentioned phenomena, dissidents compromising approximately one tenth of the world's population are missing from Confinement Centers in each Sector. Along with that number are several thousand missing person reports filed by individuals at local Control Centers in conjunction with the date of the mass disappearance. At this time our authorities have failed to identify the origin of the Orbs that filled the skies on that date, and all attempts to hinder or interrupt their operation on that date failed. Furthermore, our weapons proved useless against the hovercrafts that were involved in the actual evacuation."

"Where are the visual reports on all of this?" Maxwell asked impatiently.

"We haven't any, sir," the man said apologetically, "all attempts to record the event resulted in blank film, and even the live audio was scrambled somewhere between transmissions. All we have is static."

"Are you telling me that there isn't a shred of concrete, technical evidence that this thing ever happened?"

"That's correct. We haven't even managed to come up with a home video or even as much as a snap shot. All we have are eye witness accounts."

"Continue," Maxwell commanded shaking his head in disbelief.

"That's as far as I can go on the subject," he confessed. "We do have proof, however, that there is an organized movement of rebel troops in Russia. Much more extensive than we had previously thought and an even more recent reconnaissance of China shows up similar troop movement, but we cannot be sure if the two Sectors are involved in a coordinated effort.

"What numbers? Approximately."

"Not many. Maybe a million or two. Nothing to worry about—unless."

"Unless? Unless what?" the President demanded.

"Unless they are joined by the dissidents that disappeared."

"The dissidents were Christians not Communists," Maxwell reminded him sternly.

"Is there much difference?" he asked before continuing his report. "The Minister of Space Exploration has provided me with these provocative videos taken back in the nineties when the 'race for space' was at its height. This is the Russian Space Station that disappeared in 1992. Do you remember that incident?"

"Yes. Go on."

"The Space Station was completely capable of colonizing another planet if that had been their intent."

Maxwell laughed out loud at the suggestion.

"It *is* a possibility, sir. We are near to accomplishing the same thing today; and, I might add, if we had made it a priority years ago we would have accomplished it already!"

The Defense Minister paused, "I'm getting a live communication, Mr. President. Do you want me to receive and project it now?"

"Does it appear to apply to our investigation?"

"Yes."

"Then by all means project it."

A reporter from the Official Information Bureau appeared on the monitors, "These abandoned hovercraft have been found in many Sectors around the globe. They appear to be made of similar material and look like the ones used to evacuate the dissidents last week. We have documented eyewitness reports of men leaving the craft upon landing. The whereabouts of these persons is at this time unknown. Control Officers have been notified and at this moment are on the lookout for any suspicious movement." The transmission ended.

"This could be the breakthrough we've been looking for!" the Defense Minister exclaimed, "We need to get to those craft as soon as possible and begin weapon testing immediately."

Maxwell adjourned the meetings until the following day. The Minister of Defense left hurriedly and Maxwell went directly to the Computer Command Center beneath the Council Chamber. Paul would be tracking the incident and have up to the minute data.

"What in hell seems to be going on?" he demanded as he entered. "What have you got?"

"Things are getting more interesting by the minute, Maxwell. Look at this."

"Looks like a group of ordinary young men to me."

"Yes. But when they are stopped by Control Officers, they refused to recite. When they are scanned a curious invisible mark appears on their forehead. Look at this."

The mark, made visible by the scanner, was clearly reproduced. It was a line of strange shapes and markings that looked like a line of unfamiliar computer symbols. In the center of the series of identical symbols that were shaped like a seven was a tiny cross.

"Do they all scan?"

"Yes."

"Identical markings?"

"Yes, that's the odd part."

"Has interrogation begun? Are they willing to talk?"

"Yes. It seems that two have been singled out to represent the rest and they request an audience with you!"

"Well, by all means get them over here!"

Maxwell thought for a moment. "Bring them to me in the Temple," he said, grinning wickedly. "Bring them immediately."

Jeff, who had private quarters in the Temple, was reading in his study when Maxwell came hurriedly into the Court of Priests, "Jeff!" he shouted. "Where are you? Company is coming!"

Jeff put down his book and joined Maxwell. "What's the ruckus all about?" he asked.

Maxwell related the events of the morning: the landing of the hovercraft, the strangely marked young men, and the audience that was soon to take place.

"If there is a rebel movement to overthrow us, then perhaps these men are spies," Jeff suggested, following Maxwell up the broad marble steps to the golden throne that occupied the Holy of Holies. The arched wings of two enormous golden cherubim sheltered the throne in homage.

"I am of the same opinion," Maxwell agreed. "We'll soon discover where their loyalties lie." He sat down and Jeff stood to his side.

Two men were brought in by Control Officers to stand in the Outer Court, the Minister of Defense who was clearly distraught, accompanied them.

"President Hurst, these men claim they have been sent here on a mission of utmost importance. They say the message can only be delivered to you personally."

Maxwell, who was seated on the throne, stood up and bowed in mock greeting, "By all means," he said opening his arms wide.

The two young men, not much more than boys, stood in resolute silence. They were both handsome, one as fair as the sunlight and one of olive complexion with beautiful, dark flashing eyes.

"Come forward," Maxwell commanded. "What is your message?"

The two moved up the steps to the Court of Priests to stand before Maxwell. The fair one spoke first. "My name is Duane and my companion's name is Micah," he said in greeting. "We have been sent to command you to surrender to our King." The statement was made straight forward and without emotion.

Maxwell looked at the two puny men. He threw back his head and laughed. The sound was loud and wicked, so grotesque that even Jeff stared at his friend in wonder.

"And just who *is* your King?" he demanded.

"Jesus the Christ is our King," the men intoned as one.

Maxwell's laughter intensified and swelled as he realized that they were telling him that they were Christians, "Apparently a few got *left behind*," he thought in his exaggerated merriment.

His laughter stopped as abruptly as it began, and he leveled a dead serious look at the two men who stood before him. "I'll forgive you for that," he offered as he sat back down on the throne. "In fact I will give you a chance to redeem yourselves."

He motioned to Jeff who stepped forward and raised his arms, his splendid scarlet robes flowing down like angels wings. At once the room seemed to vibrate with a strange kind of awesome power and a bolt of brilliant lightning crashed down between the two young men who stood firm as fire leapt around their feet. Jeff's voice thundered down on them in command, "The Lord is in His Holy Temple. Let all present bow down before Him." The Control Officers and the Minister of Defense immediately fell to their knees in obedience. The other two stood in silent defiance.

Maxwell grinned at them as he pushed the button under the arm of his throne to activate the laser system. The deadly beams shot out from each direction. They seemed to scatter wildly as they bounced off their targets giving off a static hissing noise. The men still stood, their stance and gaze non-threatening but stoic. Maxwell stared back. He pressed the button a second time. "The laser must not be functioning," he thought. "Officer! Yes, you," he commanded as one of the officers looked up from the safety of the floor. "Stand up!" he demanded. The officer stood up and when he did Maxwell pushed the button for the third time. This time one head rolled to the floor with a hollow thump and the officer's body fell in a heap like a rag doll.

"That's it then," he thought, "they must have some sort of protective shield around them."

A look of pure compassion generated from the faces of the young men standing before Maxwell. "If you wish to spare your people from a worse fate than this poor man," Micah said, "then you must surrender. At this moment the Angel of Wrath is poised to pour out on your kingdom a plague of indescribable pain and suffering. You *must* surrender!"

"Lock these fools up! Don't give them any food or water until they are ready to cooperate," Maxwell commanded, rising to his feet to signify his utter contempt for their ultimatum. "We'll see who is the king around here!" Maxwell said. "We'll just see who's king!"

CHAPTER 43

"You look like death warmed over," Maxwell said, when he saw the Defense Minister the next morning.

"I feel like death warmed over," he responded. "I didn't get any sleep last night. We are dealing with something much bigger than we originally anticipated."

"What do you mean?"

"Well, whoever these people are, they have gone directly to the public. They are in every Sector, preaching the downfall of our System. Telling them to repent. What ever in hell that means!" He paused before going on to tell Maxwell that people were being urged to rebel against him personally.

Maxwell laughed, "How much influence can a handful of Communists have?"

"That's another thing, Sir. We aren't talking about a handful."

"How many?"

"We have estimated between one hundred forty to one hundred fifty thousand of them out there."

"We need answers and fast! Have the two at the Control Center brought before the Council," Maxwell ordered, "I'll delay the proceedings until you return."

When Maxwell entered, the Ministers were standing in tight little knots of intense discussion.

"Gentlemen?" Maxwell inquired. The men quickly took their places.

A very distressed Minister of Health stood to address the assembly.

"Mr. President, we have a new problem," he said. "Reports are pouring into the Department of Health of a swift moving virus sweeping the world. It begins with a single oozing sore that quickly spreads."

Maxwell's hand instinctively moved to his neck where a small sterile pad covered an oozing sore he had discovered that morning, and when he looked around the chamber at the Ministers, he realized he was not the only one affected. "My god, this *is* a fast moving virus," he thought with alarm.

"The Center for Disease Control is working on it. They know little about the virus itself, except that is spreading like wild fire."

At that moment a Control Officer entered the chamber and conferred with the Minister of Defense, who in turn came hurriedly to Maxwell.

"Did he bring the prisoners?"

The man looked embarrassed. "You aren't going to believe this, Sir, but when the Control Officer went to get them out of the cell they were gone."

"Gone?" Maxwell asked incredulously, raising his voice and drawing the attention of the other Ministers.

"Yes, gone. The cell was still locked and there didn't appear to be any way they could have escaped."

"Did they walk through the damn wall?" Maxwell demanded furiously.

"Please calm down, Mr. President. We have them," he added quickly, swallowing the saliva that collected around the growing sore inside his mouth. He could feel another one rising up on the other side and it was becoming increasingly painful to talk. "We found them talking to a crowd of people in a downtown park. The other twelve that were with them yesterday seem to have just disappeared into thin air."

"Get them in here," Maxwell growled.

The two young men were brought before the Council. Maxwell glowered down from his position above them. These two innocent looking youth represented the enemy and they would soon learn that he was an adversary not easily dealt with.

"Where are your friends?" he demanded.

"They must be about the Master's business," Micah calmly replied.

"Master? What Master? *I* am the Master of this world!" he croaked emphatically.

"Our Master is not of this world."

"Then what do you have to do with me?" Maxwell demanded.

"You must surrender."

Maxwell laughed, a mocking wicked grin creased his features. "Surrender? To whom? Your pitiful band of vagabonds?"

"To our Master."

"And if I refuse?"

"Your plagues will increase."

Maxwell unconsciously placed his hand over the gauze on his neck. "Get them out of here." He motioned for the Control Officers to come forward but the two young men turned and walked out as the Officers stood like stone soldiers unable to move or speak.

The Council of Ministers sat in stunned silence. Maxwell's thunderous voice snapped them to attention. "What are you all gaping at? Can't you see through this little *show*? The Communists have always wanted to master the world. Now they have dibs on the universe as well!"

The Ministers exchanged a puzzled look. They were at a loss to contemplate what was going on. They knew one thing, something very strange was happening, and it seemed to involve the entire population as the painful oozing sores spread throughout the entire world.

There seemed to be no way to stop the fiery 'street preachers' who stationed themselves outside the Temples every Friday, Saturday, and Sunday. "Brothers and Sisters. You must refuse to bow before President Hurst. He is not your God. It is better to lose your life in this world in exchange for life in a better world where Christ is King, a world free from pain and death, a world of love and peace."

The steady trickle of Temple executions were broadcast as a gruesome reminder of the consequences of failing to bow down on command to Maxwell Hurst, the King of the world. A war of persuasion was launched, a war of words since no other weapons were effective against these strange invaders and their awesome power.

CHAPTER 44

When they eventually dried up, the grotesque sores left scaly patches of scar tissue. The Ministry of Health was at a loss. All efforts using the latest and best medical technology had little or no effect against the hideous and painful epidemic.

Leslie's lovely face had been so scared that she refused to leave the Castle Gasbeek, choosing to seclude herself in the master suite at the top of the tower. From that lofty position she watched the treetops experience the change of seasons. She never saw her father again, and as the years rolled by, she was the fortunate one. Her isolation was a form of uneasy peace. Paul had turned into a useless, defeated shell of a man, his sole function in life being Leslie and meeting her every need.

Maxwell knew no peace. He was at the forefront of the battle. He too suffered scarring but it only enhanced his powerful and foreboding image.

Jeff had retreated into his study coming out only for Temple Instruction. He was driven to pour over ancient writings, haunted by a familiarity of recent events almost to the point of de'javu.

Once again the two dreaded young men stood before President Hurst and the Council of Ministers. They had requested an audience. Their skin was beautiful and flawless. The scourge that had so grotesquely scarred the rest of mankind had touched neither them nor any of their counterparts. Resentment and anger boiled up in Maxwell toward them. They appeared untouchable, wrapped in a secure cocoon of safety.

"You have requested permission to address the Council?"

Duane, the fair skinned youth, stepped forward. "We have been commanded to tell you that at this very moment the Angel of the Lord is pouring his bowl of wrath into the Sea, you must surrender!" His statement was neither commanding nor threatening but was rather a compassionate plea. He stepped back to stand beside his companion as if to end the audience.

"Is that all?" Maxwell asked, restraining a temptation to laugh.

Neither spoke, but as if in answer to his question, they turned and left the chamber in silence.

Maxwell fought to control his rage and it was several minutes before the mental image of their defiant backsides began to recede and he was able to continue the meeting.

In the meantime the Minister of Earth Keeping summoned a report from the Department of Water Management.

International water supply had always been a crucial issue, but for the most part the tide had been turned and with preservation and perfection of the desalinization process, the crisis had been controlled. There remained a very delicate balance, however, and the least little problem could tip the scales. He scanned the reports that were updated on a moment-to-moment basis. Suddenly a red alert appeared on the monitors and a news box popped into view. The bytes of news were transmitted and instantly converted into text. "*Alert. Major fish kill in the Mediterranean. Cause unknown.*" The first alert was replaced almost immediately, "*Alert. Major fish kill. Pacific.*"

Each Minister was glued to his monitor.

"It looks like we have another crisis," Maxwell said heavily. They all watched in horror as one report after another told of dead fish popping up in the oceans all around the globe.

In the days and weeks that followed all manpower available was thrown into the struggle. Crisis Corps worked around the clock to bury the heaps of smelly rotting flesh that continually washed up on the beaches with each new tide. Purification Plants churned around the clock to provide bottled drinking water for stricken areas. Peacekeeping Forces were disbursed wherever they were needed around the globe, assisting in the distribution of the precious liquid.

In the meantime, another ultimatum had been delivered to Maxwell and the Council. "Give up or all fresh water supplies will be polluted."

"Go to hell!" Maxwell had responded.

Maxwell knew where to find Jeff. He continued to bury himself in his study digging into ancient texts with the fervor of a possessed man.

"Jeff, why don't you get out of this hole for a while?" Maxwell asked, noticing Jeff's unkempt appearance. "You are going to rot in here. My god, Jeff, you are turning into a recluse!"

Jeff was not interested in the latest crisis, and it was obvious that Maxwell had little effect in drawing him out of himself.

"Maxwell! I am onto something *really* momentous. I can just about taste it," Jeff exclaimed with an enthusiasm that brought back memories of their far away youth when together they had planned and dreamed of a new and better world. "I can just feel it. It's like a puzzle or a riddle or something. I'm getting closer all the time. If only I can find the right piece!"

"I think the piece will be found in Russia where the Peacekeeping Force is routing out a rebel band of Communists," Maxwell stated, not willing to join in Jeff's exuberance.

"Maxwell, I want to go to Rome. The oldest theological records are in the Archives at Saint Peter's." Jeff's eyes shone with a strange expectant glow. "I'm convinced the hidden piece of the puzzle is there *somewhere*."

"Go if you must, Jeff, you are no damn good to me here. Maybe you'll discover that there are more important issues these days than burying one's self in ancient books."

The only safe drinking water to be found in the world was the frozen mountaintops of the north and south poles. It was a monumental project to melt, bottle, and ration the priceless liquid. The situation began to stabilize as the weeks and months of monotonous toiling passed by slowly.

Weekly Temple Instruction would have been a welcome break if it were not for the relentless 'messengers of doom' who remained stationed outside to preach their gospel of surrender. Week after week Maxwell's subjects entered the Temple and never failed to honor the image of their leader by bowing in obedience. If one failed to bow, he received his just reward and was silently eliminated.

CHAPTER 45

"When are you coming back to Jerusalem?" Maxwell asked the animated image of his friend on the monitor. "I miss you."

Jeff's trip to Rome had turned into a sabbatical. He was now even more reluctant to leave the cool, serene, dimly lit world of relics and books. "Soon," he promised. "I believe I've found the volumes I've been looking for. Ever hear of the Apocalypse?"

"No. What does it mean?"

"Actually it is a segment of ancient Jewish and Christian literature that has to do with divining the future. It's written in such archaic language and symbolic imagery that, frankly, it will take much more time to decipher."

"Speaking of divining the future," Maxwell said, "I've been delivered another ultimatum."

"Let me guess," Jeff offered smugly. "It concerns the sun?"

"Right."

"It's going to get hot."

"Yes."

"Hotter and hotter?"

"Yes," Maxwell said.

"You see, I told you I was on to something!"

"Maxwell laughed at Jeff's childish glee. "You are not onto anything that Environmental Management hasn't predicted. The ozone layer has been deteriorating for years. That problem has been top priority for decades, but it isn't that crucial, we'll come out on top yet!"

As the days passed, conditions worsened. The summer heat was scorching. The water crisis complicated the situation and the green earth began to turn into a brittle, brown ball of fire. Evaporated rivers became great twisting canyons. Highways to nowhere.

The harbingers of doom, and the God they claimed to serve, had become a target of hatred so intense it was almost tangible. They came and went at will and were miraculously unscathed by the problems that plagued the earth. Those thousands of healthy young men were a constant reminder to the people of their own suffering, and they cursed a God who could be so cruel, along with his so-called 'messengers'.

The Council of Ministers offered a huge reward for the head of a messenger. But people were destroyed, instead, if they attempted to harm one in any way. The Ministry of Defense, confident that a solution would be found, worked day and night to break through the shield surrounding the hovercraft. Then it would be possible to blast the shield from the army of messengers who were making war on the new system and destroying all that it had promised to be.

Breaking the shield was their only salvation. Intelligence revealed that the Communists were on the move. "If this shield is their ultimate weapon, then our System is doomed," the Defense Minister told Maxwell, "unless we can crack it before they attack."

"We've got to crack it!" Maxwell agreed. "How much time do you think we have?"

"An attack could come within the next month. They can't move a toothpick without our knowledge, not without being picked up by the scanner."

"That won't matter if the shields are still in place."

"True. That is why we *have* to disarm the shield before they can mobilize."

The Minister of Defense looked with pity at his leader. Reflecting on the last few stormy months, he said, "I don't know how you handle it. All the stress, I mean. It's been hard for all of us, but I'd sure hate to be in your shoes." Even now Maxwell seemed calm. "How do you manage to handle it?" he asked.

Maxwell smiled, a smug triumphant smile. "I have my ways," he confessed.

He did not confide his secret to the Minister. *She* had come to live with him on World Day. She filled his being. They had become one flesh. Nothing could touch him. Nothing could harm him. He was God. All he had to do was close his eyes and She was there. The ecstasy was always there.

Often he would retreat, as he did now, into the inner sanctum of the sanctuary. He would sit on the throne with closed eyes waiting to meet Her. Those times in the sanctuary were the best, when he was not the object to be venerated, but instead became a participant in pure, glorious worship.

He sat in tepid darkness spent from their union. His eyes fluttered open. He blinked several times. "I must have fallen asleep," he muttered, trying to see in the now total darkness. He groped his way toward the steps, "Why haven't the Priests lit the lamps?" A sudden thought struck him. "Perhaps the invasion has begun and we are experiencing a black out!"

All at once he stopped, knowing that he was not alone. "Who's there?" he asked in desperation, feeling his way out of the Temple. "Speak up! I know someone is here!"

"Surrender," came out of the blackness in a gentle whisper.

Maxwell fell down in dread. When he awoke, he had no idea how long he had lain unconscious in the darkness.

Indeed a deep, penetrating darkness *had* fallen upon the city of Jerusalem, but few ventured an answer as to the cause except the messengers who seemed to know everything. They claimed it was another ultimatum to surrender. Scientists claimed it was some sort of weird astronomical phenomena, but whatever the cause, it was a source of severe anxiety in Jerusalem that only added to the mounting fear of pending disaster.

A war was thought to be so eminent that Maxwell mobilized Military units from every Nation and ordered them to prepare for the defense of Jerusalem. Troops, arrived daily, setting up a mighty encampment around the city.

The Minister of Defense assured Maxwell that a breakthrough on the shield was so close it could come at any moment. Maxwell had no doubt that his forces could defeat any attack made against him, but with the ability to destroy the shield, his success would be guaranteed. The swiftness of war preparation was in itself an admirable military achievement, especially in a society where war was thought to have been obliterated.

A sense of safety pervaded Jerusalem as the military presence was made increasingly manifest throughout the area, at least until troops of another kind began to mysteriously arrive in the area. The young men who had saturated the earth with their message of doom began to gather on the hillsides outside the city walls. Their numbers swelled with alarming speed. It was evident that the two who had been the scourge of Jerusalem for over three years were in command. They had no weapons and wore no armor but the memory of past torment brought mounting fear upon the residents of the city.

The Minister of Defense came to deliver the news to Maxwell in person. "I have good news and bad news for you," he announced. "The good news is that the shield has been penetrated and a hovercraft destroyed. The bad news is that it looks like it is too late! Over one hundred thousand messengers are marching into the city at this very moment."

"What are you waiting for? Get the lasers into position. At this point we haven't got anything to lose. They have to work."

The persistent army of street preachers, who had been a source of torment for the citizens of the world, marched boldly into the courtyard of the Temple. The weapon was ready and poised for destruction. The laser performed perfectly, and what had been impossible for forty-two long months was finally accomplished as wave upon wave of the encroaching enemy were vaporized before their eyes.

"Don't vaporize those two!" Maxwell commanded. "That is too easy for them. Give them over to the people of Jerusalem. Let them have their vengeance."

And vengeance was accomplished as hundreds of people stood in line to stone the two beautiful young men to death. Maxwell refused to allow the bodies of the slain tormentors to be buried or removed from the street where they fell. News spread rapidly throughout the world. Maxwell proclaimed a three-day holiday and the massive celebration that had originally been planned for World Day was launched at last with unrestrained rejoicing. Their dead bodies became objects of scorn as throngs of people arrived to gawk and kick at the lifeless forms in bitter reproach. The scorn turned to wonder, however, as the deceased bodies showed no sign of normal corruption and the air seemed to be filled with a sweet perfume.

While Maxwell led the world in blatant revelry, a threat of a far different nature was on the move toward the Holy Land. Moving swiftly in small detachments, a huge force was being gathered in the dried up riverbed of the great Euphrates. The ever watchful sweep of the scanner, designed to identify troop movement by the craft that carried them, failed to detect the steadily enlarging army; a cavalry that was made up of flesh, blood, horses, and camels.

Chapter 46

Jeff arrived back in Jerusalem in time for the celebration. He had the apocalyptic books in tow along with a strange looking small gold chest. "I have solved the puzzle!" he exclaimed, "Now we can beat them at their own game!"

"Are you the only person in the world who hasn't heard the good news? We have already beaten them," Maxwell said. "The enemy has been destroyed."

"One hundred and forty four thousand dead Jews *do not* represent the enemy," Jeff stated, spreading the books out before Maxwell. "Those men were merely spouting what they knew was written here, in what they considered sacred writings. No, there is a force much greater than they."

"The Communists?" Maxwell offered.

"Greater than that." Jeff directed Maxwell's attention to a specific portion of the prophetic writings. "Look at this list of events, seven in all. They are a series of crises that exactly match the horrors of the past three years."

Maxwell read the passages with growing disbelief. "How can this be possible?", he wondered out loud.

"Amazing isn't it? But look at this." Jeff took the book and read, "The sixth angel poured out his vial upon the great River Euphrates, and the water thereof was dried up, that the way of the Kings of the east might be prepared. And I saw three unclean spirits like frogs come out of the mouth of the dragon and out of the mouth of the beast and out of the mouth of the false prophet. For they are the spirits of devils, working miracles, which go forth unto the Kings of the earth and of the whole world, to gather them to the battle on that great day of God Almighty. Behold I come as a thief. Blessed is he that watcheth, and keepeth his garments, lest he walk naked, and they see his shame. And he gathered them together into a place called in the Hebrew tongue Armageddon."

"Now *that*, I can't understand," Maxwell confessed.

"That's because it hasn't happened yet. You understand the others, the sores, the fish kill, the sunburn, and the darkness because you experienced it. We *all* experienced it. Those events are part of our past. Yours and mine," Jeff explained. "What we need to do is lift out what we do understand and try to decipher the rest."

"Decipher away," Maxwell invited, "I'm all ears."

"Well, number one, we know the Euphrates was pretty much drained during the great earthquake and what was left probably evaporated during the scorching heat of last summer."

"I can go along with that."

"Second, we are certain that Russia and China are planning an invasion at some time in the very near future."

"Agreed."

"Third, we know that Armageddon is the Hebrew word for Megiddo and that somebody's armies are going to be gathered there for a great battle."

"I'll take your word for that."

"The rest isn't as easy. The dragon, the beast, and the false prophet seem to represent some great opposing force," Jeff ventured, "perhaps a force opposing our own System of Government."

"The Communists!"

"Perhaps."

"You don't sound very convincing. Who or what else on earth could it possibly mean? We have no other enemies."

While Jeff was secluded at the Vatican, it seemed clear to him that the world was caught in the vice of some great, cosmic, spiritual battle, a war between good and evil, but now everything was getting fuzzy in his mind. "I guess you're right. I've read so much of this stuff that it's confusing my brain."

"I wonder what it will do to the Defense Minister's brain when I tell him all this. He'll think I'm nuts when I suggest that we move our troops to Megiddo."

"If he isn't convinced by the predictions in this book and their authenticity, then I have a little ace in the hole," Jeff grinned patting the small gold box.

"What's in that box, anyway?" Maxwell asked with growing curiosity.

Jeff picked up the box and opened the lid.

"Ever hear of Fatima?"

"Fatima?" Maxwell searched for the distant, familiar word.

"Yes. Yes, of course, now I remember. Fatima is a place in Portugal where some children were supposed to have seen visions of the Virgin Mary years ago, nineteen sixteen, or was it seventeen? What about it?"

"The vision was given in three parts. The first and second were revealed in their time, but a third known as the 'third secret of Fatima' was never revealed. Instructions were given by Sister Lucia that the 'third part of the secret' could only be revealed after 1960, but Pope John XXIII after reading it made the decision to return the prophesy to its place in this box. Again, in 1965, another Pope called for the box; he also read the prophesy it contained and decided not to publish it. It was only after the assassination attempt on the life of Pope John Paul II in 1981 that the 'secret' was made public. There is a slight problem, however; the text of the revealed 'secret' of 1981 does not appear to be the same text as the one found in this box."

Jeff took out the brittle, yellowed hand written document; it was dated July 19, 1917. "It is written in Portuguese, but I took the liberty of getting it translated into English." He handed a copy to Maxwell.

"What has this got to do with us?"

"Read it," Jeff urged.

"At the time of the end, a great leader shall fall, brought down by a fatal wound to the head, or so it will seem. He will be carried away into the wilderness where he will be nurtured and cared for by My Immaculate Heart. Afterward he will be made manifest and save the lives of many."

"Notice the date when it was told to the child Lucia by the Virgin Mary in the Cova da Iria, July, 1917. Now look at this; this is the statement that was sealed up with the original letter by Pope John. Look at the date."

Maxwell fixed his eyes on the dates. It was the year of his assassination. The prophecy foretold his own role in history.

"Can you just imagine what the press would have made out of this at the time?" Jeff asked. "Our clandestine operation would have been fruitless, fueled with this information."

It all began to make sense. Everything!

Maxwell commanded the Minister of Defense to immediately move his Peacekeeping Forces into Megiddo, the great pass that connected the coastal plain and the Plain of Esdraelon, to prepare for the defense of Jerusalem.

CHAPTER 47

"**This unrestricted carousing** has gone on long enough." Maxwell told Jeff referring to the three-day celebration in the streets of Jerusalem. "It's time to get back to business. Broadcast a Public Announcement that we will incinerate at three this afternoon. Afterward we will leave for Megiddo."

News of the incineration spread rapidly throughout the city and people began to gather long before three, eager to get one last look at the objects of contempt. The bodies of the two beautiful young men were still as perfect and virgin as their lives had been, in spite of the fact that they had been punched, prodded, and kicked repeatedly while they lay exposed on the Jerusalem street.

The world wide live broadcast of the incineration would bring the festivities to a grand finale. People gathered in Temples in every Sector to view the event.

"Bring the two that troubled Jerusalem to me," Maxwell ordered. "I want them brought to me here," he motioned to the area just below the Throne where he sat in authority.

Everything was done as Maxwell commanded and at three o'clock the bodies of the two men lay on the marble floor before him. Control Officers were in place and ready to begin incineration. At Maxwell's signal, the lasers were aimed and fired. The weapons pumped out a pulse of light that seemed to shimmer around the two prostrate figures. Maxwell looked at Jeff in amazement.

Another pulse was fired. A clap of thunder sent Maxwell up to his feet from the Throne, and he looked around at Jeff in fear. A second rumble of thunder started low and seemed far in the distance but got louder and louder until the Temple began to vibrate. Suddenly a brilliant light, not from the laser, surrounded the two men on the floor bathing them in an iridescent glow. Maxwell watched in terror as the two men began to stir, stretching as though just awakening from a peaceful sleep. They stood up, still encased in the beautiful light. A white mist seemed to completely envelope them. The mist rose slowly toward the ceiling, and when it cleared, they were gone.

"I've never seen a laser work like that!" exclaimed the Control Officer in wonder.

Jeff stood in total shock and Maxwell was fighting hard to regain his composure. A third and final clap of thunder sounded, sending them all tumbling to the floor. Screams echoed forth from the people outside as the marble courts where they stood disappeared beneath them. The walls of the Temple began to sway and crack.

"We gotta get out of here!" Jeff yelled.

The two men ran from the building with the chaotic crowd trying to evacuate the Temple Grounds. Maxwell was reduced to a mere man running for his life, pushing and shoving his way toward the Palace. Huge hail rained down upon the city. Hail so huge that many people in the city were killed instantly.

"Stay under the portico," Maxwell shouted to Jeff.

Jeff looked dubious, not knowing how long before the huge columns would crumble down upon them.

The pilot was waiting in the hovercraft. He had initiated the protective shield to ward off the hordes of people trying to board. When he saw Maxwell and Jeff under the Portico, he lifted the hovercraft gently and picked them up. Seconds after they were inside, the craft lifted up and away from the awful destruction.

This earthquake, far more devastating than the last one, left three huge gaping fissures grinning fiendishly up at them. The last thing they saw was the splendid Temple crumbing in an explosive heap.

Maxwell threw back his head and let out a howl that reverberated around the world as the scene was repeated over and over again when one Temple after another came crashing down.

"Get us out of here. Quick!" Jeff demanded.

Maxwell sat in stunned silence as the hovercraft headed for Megiddo, flying high above the destruction. "Look!" he croaked, pointing downward. The Euphrates riverbed was clearly visible below them.

Jeff strained to see what Maxwell saw.

"Down there!" he said again. This time Jeff saw what seemed to be the river bed filled with a moving sea of water, but as the hovercraft swept lower it was apparent that what looked like a wave of blue water surging from the north was in fact an army of tremendous proportions.

"The Communists!" Maxwell shouted. "Get me to Megiddo. Fast!"

When they arrived at Megiddo, the General and his forces were running in six different directions trying to restore order following the earthquake. The hail had taken a heavy toll and hundreds of men lay in rank and file on the ground.

"The enemy is approaching from the South. They are marching up out of the Euphrates river bed at this very moment," Maxwell told the bewildered General. "You must prepare for a defense."

The General looked around at his disoriented troops, "How soon will they get here?" he asked.

"They are only a day's march away, at the most."

"I can't be ready by then!" the General stated in alarm.

"You can and you will, damn it," Maxwell thundered back.

Jeff who hadn't slept in over forty-eight hours was receding further and further into himself. Images of horror danced in constant replay at the back of his eyeballs. He fell backwards and lay senseless staring up into the heavens.

"They're coming, they're coming," Jeff screamed pointing toward the sky. Every eye looked heavenward and saw the great shinning Orbs descending toward the earth.

"Come on!" Maxwell motioned, jumping up and down like a madman. "Come on, you sons-of-bitches." He tried to pull Jeff to his feet. "Get up, you bastard! Get up and fight like a man. We broke the shield. We'll blow them right out of the sky!"

The general looked around at his pitiful army. "Fat chance," he thought.

The Orbs moved closer. Suddenly one dropped lower than the rest. It appeared to be preparing to land. It was so close that the men could see the brilliant, white glimmer of its underside. At the same time a mighty shout arose from the south as a hoard of mounted men in blue and yellow armor thundered across the plain toward Maxwell's position. They were caught. Trapped from below and above.

Maxwell fell to his knees. "Holy Mary, Mother of God," he prayed. He looked up. *She* was there! When had she ever failed him? The beautiful apparition stood between him, the Orb, and the chaos that surrounded him. He stood to his feet and shook his fist toward heaven.

At that moment two things happened at once. The earth was rent beneath their feet and fire rained down from the Orb killing everything it touched- horse, rider, generals, and soldiers from the greatest to the least. Maxwell and Jeff, unhurt but shaken, lay on the ground beneath the silent, hovering Orb. They stood up amid the deadly silence of the battlefield.

"What's that sound?" Maxwell whispered.

"I don't know, but it's getting louder."

"My god, look at that!"

A great flock of squawking, swooping birds descended on the plains where dead bodies lay strewn like seeds upon a fertile field. The advancing army of birds began to peck and pull at the two men, pulling away great chunks of flesh. Blood steamed down their faces as they ran screaming in pain. They didn't see the great crevice that stood in their path. Maxwell had little time to expel the scream that clutched his throat as he and Jeff fell headlong into the deep fiery pit, followed by a blue, misty shape, much like a woman's.

The earth trembled and heaved one more time as the gaping jaws of the fissure were closed behind them.

END

EPILOUGE

As the Puppet Prince comes to an end Maxwell Hurst has met his demise, or
so it seems. A friend asked me, after she had read my manuscript, "Where do
you come up with all this stuff?" My inspiration is found between the covers
of the Bible. From Old Testament prophesies found in the Books of Ezekiel
and Daniel to the New Testament, especially Matthew 24 and the book of
Revelation. My first book, The Sign, and this one, The Puppet Prince, are
framed within these scriptures. The conspiracy surrounding the Antichrist
(Revelation Chapter 13) who has a head wound that appears to be fatal?
Yes, I must admit mirrors our beloved JFK. The Angels' gospel message
(Matthew 24:14 and Revelation 14:6-12) is a phenomenal world-wide event.
The Orbs that portray my Angels are patterned after the wheel within the
wheel in Chapter One of Ezekiel. When the Antichrist presents himself in the
Temple as God (Matthew 24:15) the great tribulation is portrayed as a flood
in Jerusalem that impacts the whole world. (Daniel 9:26-27 and Matthew
24:16-22) The evacuation of the faithful who have endured to the end is
found in Revelation14:14-16. The 144,000 evangelists who preach to those
"left behind" and the "7 bowls of wrath" are found in Revelation Chapters
14,15, and 16. Revelation 17,18, and 19 gave me divine inspiration for the great
harlot and her false religion. Revelation 19:17-21 brings my main characters
to an end when Maxwell, who portrays the Antichrist, Jeff who represents

the one world religion, and the Queen of Heaven who represents the unholy spirit, are swallowed into the bowels of the earth.

The Millennium begins. (Revelation 20:1-3)

Another Book? My divine imagination is at work!

Made in the USA
Columbia, SC
02 July 2017